Our Covenant of Prosperity

Crossing the Threshold
to Supernatural Abundance

by

Markus Bishop

HARRISON HOUSE
Tulsa, Oklahoma

Unless otherwise indicated, all Scripture quotations are taken from the *King James Version* of the Bible.

2nd Printing

Our Covenant of Prosperity:
Crossing the Threshold to Supernatural Abundance
ISBN 0-89274-991-1
Copyright © 1997 by Markus Bishop
P. O. Box 14121
Panama City Beach, Florida 32413

Published by Harrison House, Inc.
P. O. Box 35035
Tulsa, Oklahoma 74153

Contents

Foreword

by
Kenneth Copeland

This book is a powerful tool that the Lord has provided to help you gain the breakthroughs you need financially. Not just momentary financial fixes from time to time to help you get through to the end of the month — I'm talking about major breakthroughs. Breakthroughs that bring heaven down and into your whole financial life.

To those of you who are just now finding out that it is actually God's will for you to prosper, Brother Bishop's straightforward, line-on-line style of writing will help you study your Bible on this wonderful subject, and build a sound biblical foundation for your faith to stand on. For those who have already begun to learn and lean on Jesus' ways in your financial life, this book is exciting and ever so revealing of the heart of our wonderful Father who wants to surround us with our most wonderful dreams.

As always, Markus sticks strictly to the written Word. That's one of the things I like so much about his teaching and writing. He's a man of faith and a stickler for God's Word in his own life. He preaches the way he lives and he lives the way he preaches. It really comes through in this wonderful book. It will serve you, the reader, and help you to truly "cross the threshold to supernatural abundance."

Introduction

Is it really God's will for His people to prosper financially?

This question has caused arguments and debates for years throughout the Body of Christ.

Fewer subjects have been fought over more than the teaching of financial prosperity. Nothing can stir up more devils, or insult more tradition, or offend more religious thinking, or catch more persecution.

Yet, according to God's Word, it is God's will for His people to be prosperous. All the arguments against it do not change the promises of God's Word. The Word clearly promises that financial prosperity is a blessing from the Lord for *every* believer. This truth should be preached so that God's people can be set free.

Many good people would never ask God for prosperity, because religious tradition says that it's wrong for them to be financially prosperous. But that's not what the Word of God says.

In this study we will be examining this subject of financial prosperity from the authority of God's Word. We will find out what God's Word has to say about poverty and lack. It is my desire to kill a few sacred cows and barbecue a few traditions.

I believe this is a strategic and timely study into some powerful passages of Scripture about your authority as a believer in God's kingdom and the principles involved in

His Covenant. Receiving from God and His Word is not like driving through a fast-food window. God's Word isn't like fast food. You have to take time to chew on it, feed on it and meditate on it.

I pray that this study will be a blessing to your life as you learn what God's Word has to say about your covenant of prosperity. God has promised blessings to those who will receive His covenant principles. As you operate according to these principles, you will experience supernatural abundance in your life.

1

Prosperity — It *Is* God's Will!

Let's look at some passages of Scripture showing God's will for His Church to be blessed.

> Moreover, brethren, we do you to wit (or we desire you to know) of the *grace* of God bestowed on the churches of Macedonia;
>
> How that in a great trial of affliction the abundance of their joy and their deep poverty abounded unto the riches of their liberality (or giving).
>
> Therefore, *as ye abound in every thing,* in faith, and utterance, and knowledge, and in all diligence, and in your love to us, see that ye abound in this *grace* also.
>
> I speak not by commandment, but by occasion of the forwardness of others, and to prove the sincerity of your love.
>
> For ye know the *grace* of our Lord Jesus Christ, that, though he was rich, yet for your sakes *he became poor, that ye through his poverty might be rich.*
>
> 2 Corinthians 8:1,2,7-9

The word *grace* traditionally has been defined as God's unmerited favor, but that is a limited part of its definition. In light of the Scriptures, God's grace is really an empowering of God's ability in your life.

9

The apostle Paul was saying to the Church, "I want you to know something supernatural that is taking place at the churches of Macedonia."

Those believers were living in the midst of a horrible economy. They were being faced with many challenges and attacks financially, yet they were abounding in their giving to the work of God.

Paul, writing by inspiration of the Holy Spirit, was saying, "I desire that this same supernatural ability would abound in your church."

The Blessing of Abraham

Another portion of Scripture I want us to read is taken from Galatians, chapter 3. Paul is not talking here about something the Lord Jesus Christ will attempt to do one day or promises He will do in the future. He is referring to something Jesus has *already* done. Let's begin with verse 13:

> *Christ hath redeemed us from the curse of the law,* being made a curse for us: for it is written, Cursed is every one that hangeth on a tree:

> That the *blessing of Abraham* might come on the Gentiles through Jesus Christ; that we might receive the promise of the Spirit through faith.

> Galatians 3:13,14

Now in verse 14 it does not say that we would become recipients of God's promising us the Spirit, but rather that we might receive the promise which the Holy Spirit made through the Word of God. Then it tells us in verses 28 and 29:

> There is neither Jew nor Greek, there is neither bond nor free, there is neither male nor female: for ye are all one in Christ Jesus.

> And if ye be Christ's, then are ye Abraham's seed, and *heirs according to the promise.*

10

Jesus Became Poor for You

I want us to look again at Second Corinthians, chapter 8, verse 9. This Scripture teaches that Jesus Christ has purchased for us through His own sacrifice not only the right but the redemptive promise of being prosperous. It says:

For ye know the grace of our Lord Jesus Christ, that, though he was rich, yet for your sakes he became poor.

Do you understand how rich Jesus was before He left heaven? He was sitting on the throne of God and walking on streets of gold. In the book of Revelation we see Jesus coming to talk to the apostle John. He didn't appear wearing old clothes; He had on white raiment. There wasn't just a band of gold on His finger; His chest was covered with a vest of pure gold. (Rev. 1:13-16.)

Jesus was experiencing the wealth of heaven, but He left all of that to come down to earth. He was not born in some fancy place, but in a barn. He experienced poverty until He entered the ministry and began through His faith to exercise the laws of abundance and prosperity.

Yet notice Second Corinthians 8:9 says that He, for your sake, became poor.

You might ask, *Why did He do that?*

To set an example for you.

An example of how I am to be poor and humble and lowly in heart?

No. So that you, through His poverty, might be rich.

I think many people miss this. They say, "Well, Jesus didn't have anything, so we shouldn't have anything, either." The point is, He had *everything*, but He relinquished it for a season to come to earth as a man and

11

pay for our poverty of spirit, soul and body. He took our poverty in exchange for His riches.

Prosperity Is a Part of Your Redemption

Jesus was made poor that you, through His poverty, might be rich.

After looking up each word of Second Corinthians 9:8 in Greek, I found that, in the original text of the epistles from the apostle Paul, these words deal specifically with financial prosperity. Yes, Jesus died on the cross and rose again that you might be born again and be in right standing before God; but He also bought and paid for prosperity that you might walk in the fullness of it.

Financial prosperity has to be seen for what it scripturally is: a part of your redemption in Christ Jesus, something Jesus paid for on the cross. His suffering purchased it for you.

Your Prosperity Pleases God

God absolutely takes pleasure in your being prosperous. Psalm 35:27 says He **hath pleasure in the prosperity of his servant.** Are you willing to please God by being prosperous?

This entire verse from Psalm 35 says:

> **Let them shout for joy, and be glad, that favour my righteous cause** (in other words, those who are on God's side)**: yea, let them say continually, Let the Lord be magnified,** *which hath pleasure in the prosperity of his servant.*

Some people read it this way:

> *Let them shout for joy, and be glad, that favor my righteous cause: yea, let them say continually, God wants me broke.*

But that's not what this verse of Scripture says. Again, it says:

...let them say continually, Let the Lord be magnified, which hath pleasure in the prosperity of his servant.

God wants to see His people prosper. Under the Old Covenant, the Israelites were servants of God who brought **pleasure** to the heart of God through their prosperity. How much more today do we as believers, as sons and daughters of God, as children of the Most High God, bring pleasure to the heart of God when we do well financially?

This Scripture is saying, "Let God be magnified, let us say continually that God wants us blessed!" We need to always be saying that God wants us to prosper.

The children in our church have presented some wonderful music, singing about how God is good. But how can God be good if He doesn't want us to be financially blessed? As Jesus said: **If ye then, being evil, know how to give good gifts unto your children, how much more shall your Father which is in heaven give good things to them that ask him?** (Matt. 7:11).

Let's think of ourselves in comparison to the goodness of God. We fall far below God's goodness. As parents, we are always trying to help our children and bless them. We desire that they would prosper and have lots of good things. Then how much more does our heavenly Father give good things to those who ask Him?

When you receive a bill in the mail, your first question should not be, "How am I going to pay it?" Your first question should be, "I wonder how my heavenly Father is going to bring it to me this time?"

The Blessing of the Lord

Proverbs 10:22 refers to the blessing of the Lord. It says:

The blessing of the Lord, it maketh rich....

As a child of God, a joint-heir with Jesus Christ, you have been given the blessing of the Lord. The blessings of Abraham are already yours. (Rom. 8:17; Gal. 3:14.)

As believers, we become enriched in our souls when we know the Lord. The word *rich* in this verse from Proverbs is the Hebrew word pronounced "aw-shar´."[1] It has only one meaning, and that is for financial prosperity. It is a word that describes wealth, money, income. It has nothing to do with anything like virtue or good feeling.

You could quote Proverbs 10:22 this way: "The blessing of the Lord, it maketh financial prosperity."

Verse 22 goes on to say:

...and he addeth no sorrow with it.

God has a system, but the world has a system, too. In fact, the world's system is vicious. It can bring prosperity to people, but sorrow goes along with it. The prosperity of God's system comes without sorrow.

A Blessing to *Every* Believer

In the New Testament we find where God's Word clearly, without a shadow of a doubt, promises financial prosperity as a blessing from God for every believer.

The Third Epistle of John, verse 2, begins with this salutation: **Beloved....** Because you are a born-again

---

[1]James H. Strong. *Strong's Exhaustive Concordance.* Compact Ed. (Grand Rapids: Baker, 1992), "Hebrew and Chaldee Dictionary," p. 92, #6238.

Christian, this epistle is God speaking to you. It says, **Beloved, I wish....** In the Greek, another meaning for the word *wish* is the word *will*.[2] Here in verse 2, God is telling us His will for His people. He says:

> **Beloved, I wish (or will) above all things that thou mayest prosper and be in health, even as thy soul prospereth.**

If it's God's will for every believer to prosper, then why are so many dear Christian brothers and sisters still experiencing poverty and lack? Because their soul has not been trained in this truth. Their understanding of the Scriptures has not been renewed to include all the promises of God. You will prosper in accordance with your understanding of the Word and your obedience to that Word.

It's not just having a covenant with God; it's being a doer of the Word that releases these blessings. But if you don't know the Word, how can you be a doer of the Word? You will only prosper in proportion to the prosperity of your soul, or your understanding of the Scriptures.

You have to understand that it's God's will for everybody to be saved, yet people are burning in hell this very moment. Some people are in hell because no one ever told them about the Lord Jesus Christ. Others are there because they rejected what had been told them concerning the Lord.

The same is true regarding financial prosperity. There are many Christians who don't know anything about financial prosperity as a promise from the Lord in His Word. Others have rejected it, thinking it is wrong.

Nonetheless, it is God's will for you, as His child, to be prosperous. We must establish, beyond a shadow of a doubt, that God desires for you to prosper.

---

[2]Strong, "Greek Dictionary of the New Testament," p. 34, #2172.

Knowing God's Will

Prosperity is just like any promise, any blessing or any other provision of your redemption in God through Christ Jesus. You have a right to divine prosperity. But before it will ever become a reality in your life, you have to be totally convinced that it's for you. You have to know that you know that you know that prosperity is the will of God for your life.

Maybe you know for a fact that, were you to die right now, you would miss hell and go to heaven. With that same assurance of your salvation, you need to know that it is God's will for you to be financially prosperous.

I remember some wonderful words shared by Rev. Kenneth E. Hagin in a meeting several years ago. They were so powerfully true; I can't improve upon them. He said, "Faith can never rise above the known will of God."

God's Word says:

> **And this is the confidence that we have in him, that, if we ask any thing according to his will, he heareth us:**
>
> **And if we know that he hear us, whatsoever we ask, we know that we have the petitions that we desired of him.**
>
> **1 John 5:14,15**

Knowledge of the will of God is so important for you to have faith in your prayers. You can't believe for something when you don't know if it's God's will for you to receive it.

When you know it's God's will for you to be saved, you have faith to be saved.

When you know it's God's will for you to be healed, you can feed your spirit with promises of divine healing from God's Word and have faith to be healed.

Of course, learning how to release that faith is yet another aspect of appropriating the promise. Whenever there is a doubt concerning healing being the will of God, then there will be lack of faith in bringing it to pass.

By the same principle, you have to know beyond any doubt that God wants you to prosper. If you don't know whether it's God's will for you to be financially prosperous, you will never be praying in faith. You will never be praying with the aggressiveness necessary to actually transfer wealth out of the kingdom of darkness and into the hands of God's people in these last days.

Stirring Up the Devil

Have you ever noticed how sensitive people are about their money? You can talk to them about the way they look, the way they talk, even about their family. But when you start talking about their money, you get onto another level.

Money seems to be where people really live. The truth is, they are that way about money, because that's how the devil is about money.

When you start talking about money, you really stir up the devil! You have to understand that he is **the god of this world** (2 Cor. 4:4). But he is not God of the earth. Scripture says, **The earth is the Lord's, and the fulness thereof** (1 Cor. 10:26). But he is god of the world's system.

When you start talking about the prosperity of believers, you are talking about money being taken out of the devil's pocket. That money comes from his operation, his kingdom, and it's put over into the kingdom of God to help pay for the Gospel being preached throughout the world. That makes him mad!

The devil loves money. The Bible says, **The love of money is the root of all evil** (1 Tim. 6:10). Not money itself, but the *love* of it. You can commit that sin without a dime in your pocket!

God Wants You To Prosper!

There is some perverted preaching going on in the pulpits of America and all over the world that says God wants His people to be poor. That idea does not even align itself with the Scriptures nor with the nature and character of God.

People's minds have been so cluttered with garbage that they can't even think straight. They think, *Well, I'm having a financial difficulty. God must be trying to teach me something.* The only thing God wants to teach His people is how to be prosperous and lead other people to Jesus Christ.

Financial prosperity is not to be viewed as just some positive-thinking opportunity that God will allow you to get mixed up in. It is not something God will tolerate your involvement with, like some kind of social club.

Financial prosperity has to be seen for what it scripturally and actually is: a part of your redemption, which Jesus Christ died and paid for. You have to see prosperity in that light. It's not an option. It's not something God just tolerates or allows you to have in His permissive will.

But some people have that perception of prosperity. That would be like having some kind of business which God just allows you to have. God's prosperity is more than that.

Prosperity is one of the things the precious blood of Jesus was shed to purchase for you. You need to renew your mind to this truth. Prosperity was bought and paid for by Jesus Christ. It is the perfect will of God for your life. God wants you to prosper!

2

Redeemed From
the Curse of Poverty

We previously read a passage of Scripture from Galatians, chapter 3. Again, verse 13 says:

> **Christ hath redeemed us from the curse of the law....**

To be honest with you, after I had been attending church for nineteen years, I had no earthly idea what this Scripture was talking about. I was going to church services and other church activities three or four times a week. But I wasn't saved; I was just being religious. So this Scripture verse meant nothing whatsoever to me at that time.

Again, it says:

> **Christ hath redeemed us from the curse of the law, being made a curse for us....**

Jesus suffered for us while hanging on that cross. Why did He do this? The verse goes on:

> **...for it is written, Cursed is every one that hangeth on a tree** (or on the cross)**:**
>
> **That the blessing of Abraham might come on the Gentiles through Jesus Christ; that we might receive the promise of the Spirit through faith.**
>
> **Galatians 3:13,14**

You see, the curse of the Law involved complete and total separation from God and all of His blessings. It had to do with death and with the curse of sickness, disease, depression and oppression; but it also dealt with the curse of poverty.

Poverty Is a Curse

Do you understand that poverty is a curse? There is nothing blessed about being poor. There is no godly virtue in suffering lack. In fact, poverty is contrary to every plan or purpose of God for your life, and it will keep you from doing the will of God. Poverty is not a blessing or a spiritual virtue or some sign of spirituality. It has nothing whatsoever to do with holiness or being like God. God is not poor!

There was only one reason Jesus ever experienced any poverty in His life. It was not to set an example for you, but rather to pay the price so that you could be free from it. He became poor in order to suffer and purchase this redemption for you, redeeming you from the curse of the Law, which included poverty.

You can even say it this way: "Jesus redeemed me from poverty so that the blessing of Abraham might come upon me."

God Made a Covenant With Abraham

Many times Jews are made fun of by other people because of their wealth. Some offensive terms are used. For example, it is said that they will work at "jewing down" another person on the price of some item.

This covenant all started when God appeared to Abram. God changed his name to Abraham and told him how blessings would come upon him. (See Gen. 17.)

No matter where Abraham went or what he did, he would prosper because he had made a covenant, or contract, with God. This covenant promised that, if he would serve God, he could even move to another country, leaving behind everything he had, and God would supernaturally prosper him, even in the middle of a famine.

Jesus bought and paid for you to be able to receive this blessing of Abraham. The Word of God teaches that He has redeemed us from this curse of financial poverty or lack just like He redeemed us from everything else. In fact, financial prosperity is just as much a part of the Gospel of Jesus Christ as being born again and washed in His blood.

The Curse of the Law

I want to quote Galatians 3:13 again. It says:

> **Christ hath redeemed us from the curse of the law, being made a curse for us....**

Let's learn some things about this curse of the Law. It is found in Deuteronomy, chapter 28. The books of Genesis through Deuteronomy are referred to as "the Law." This is also called the Law of Moses; it was the Law of God as given by the Holy Ghost to the prophet Moses.

Deuteronomy 28 may not mean much to the mind of the Western Christian, but those who are in covenant with God know about the curse of the Law. The Jew who walked after God's covenant in those days really understood the curse.

This curse begins in verse 15:

> **But it shall come to pass, if thou wilt not hearken unto the voice of the Lord thy God, to observe to do all his commandments and his statutes which I command thee this day; that all these curses shall come upon thee, and overtake thee.**

Then beginning in verse 16 all these curses are given. Let's look at some aspects of this curse of the Law.

Oppression

Notice verse 33, which says:

> **The fruit of thy land, and all thy labours, shall a nation which thou knowest not eat up; and thou shalt be only oppressed and crushed alway.**

This means God's people would be under the financial oppression of another nation, that everything they do would be consumed by others, that they would be unable to enjoy the fruit of their own labors.

Financial Disaster

Verse 38 says:

> **Thou shalt carry much seed out into the field, and shalt gather but little in; for the locust shall consume it.**

This part of the curse tells how people's investments will be devoured, bearing no fruit or increase. It goes on to talk about this in verse 44:

> **He** (the stranger, the enemy) **shall lend to thee, and thou shalt not lend to him: he shall be the head, and thou shalt be the tail.**

This verse describes God's people being under financial obligation to a strange nation or person. To us today this would mean being under the domination of the world's system. That's a part of the curse of the Law.

But as we read in Galatians 3:13, Christ has redeemed us from the curse of the Law, which means He has redeemed us from poverty and from the world's dominion over our finances.

Poverty Is Contrary to God

Never has poverty been a part of God's desire for His people. In fact, poverty is contrary to the very nature of our heavenly Father. Poverty and God just don't go together.

I want to share with you a definition of the word *poor*. Some people don't really know what it means; they just think it means not having any money. According to Webster's dictionary, *poor* means "having little or no means to support one's self or others; lacking in quality and productivity; being inferior; lacking pleasure, comfort or satisfaction in life."

Scripture after Scripture clearly opposes any and all aspects of the words *poor* or *poverty*. God's Word contradicts this idea of always doing without. God's will is for His people to have all sufficiency in all things so that we can abound unto *every* good work. (2 Cor. 9:8.)

God doesn't want you to be poor. He wants you to be blessed and to be a blessing to others.

Jesus said, "I have come that you might have life and have it more abundantly." (John 10:10.) That means having a quality of life — the God-kind of life.

Poverty is nowhere near abundant living; it means just existing. God didn't come just so you would be able to exist; He came for you to have abundance in this life. According to the Word of God, poverty is not God's will. Poverty is lacking productivity.

In John 15:8 Jesus said that the Father takes pleasure when you produce fruit. This occurs through receiving answered prayer and having God's blessings in your life. God wants you to produce; He doesn't want you to be poor. Poverty is being inferior.

The Bible says: **If any man be in Christ, he is a new creature: old things are passed away; behold, all things are become new** (2 Cor. 5:17). All the things we become in Christ are of God. That is not inferiority; it is superiority to the world's system and to the carnal, unregenerated man, which you were before you came to know Christ.

God doesn't want you to be poor or to be lacking pleasure, comfort or satisfaction in your life. First Timothy 6:17 says God **giveth us richly all things to enjoy.** Scripture after Scripture clearly opposes any and all aspects of the word *poor*. But that can be difficult for people to receive. It's hard sometimes on the flesh and on the religious mind.

If you are poor, if you lack prosperity and are experiencing poverty, then you are not in God's perfect will. That doesn't mean you are a sinner; it just means you are not in the *perfect* will of God.

Salvation Includes Prosperity

In the book of Romans, chapter 1, verse 16, the apostle Paul, writing by inspiration of the Holy Spirit, says this:

> **For I am not ashamed of the gospel of Christ: for it is the power of God unto salvation to every one that believeth....**

Dr. C. I. Scofield in his edition of the Bible has some great notes. There are some particular parts of his commentary that are powerful. I would just like to quote Dr. Scofield's notes regarding this portion of Scripture. He says:

> "The Hebrew and Greek words for *salvation* imply the ideas of deliverance, safety, preservation, healing and soundness."[1]

---

[1]*Scofield Edition Reference Bible*. Commentary Notes. (Grand Rapids, Michigan: World Publishing, 1917), p. 1192.

That's what the Word of God has to say about it.

You may say, "But I don't believe in prosperity." Then you don't know what God's Word says.

You see, salvation doesn't just mean being recreated in your spirit; it has to do with every aspect of your life — spirit, soul, body, financially and socially.

Salvation even includes the redemption of your own family out of the devil's hand. The curse of the Law includes all kinds of family problems, like going through a divorce and having children on drugs. Christ has redeemed you so that you don't have to have all that family turmoil.

So it's time for you to stand up and say no to the devil. You may say, "Well, that's not a part of what God has done for us." Yes, it is. Jesus came **that he might destroy the works of the devil** (1 John 3:8).

Rejecting Knowledge

You might ask, "If financial prosperity is just as much a part of the Gospel of Jesus Christ as being born again, why are so many dear Christian brothers and sisters experiencing poverty and lack?"

The answer, very simply, is found in the book of Hosea. Chapter 4, verse 6, tells us that God's people perish for a lack of knowledge. But it goes on to say that they have rejected knowledge.

This is where many Christians are today. They have heard the Word of God about prosperity, but reject it because it demands something of them. Having any blessing of God in your life is going to require something on your part. But laziness or an unwillingness to apply yourself certainly will rob you of many of God's blessings.

Lots of people just don't know about prosperity. After I had heard the good Word of God, I found out that God was for me, not against me. That's when I got born again. But I didn't know about prosperity at the time. In fact, I answered the call to preach thinking that was synonymous with a vow of poverty.

So, some people suffer because of a lack of knowledge. Others, like those involved in religion, will hear the message of prosperity and then work hard to fight against it.

One day I had lunch with the pastor of a denominational church in Alabama. He said to me: "I am so frustrated with my denomination. The people just want to kill the Word of God. Every time we find a beautiful promise of victory, they are always trying to explain it away."

Don't ever explain away the promises of God; receive them.

You see, some people want to reject God's Word. If they ever admit that it's true, they will have to explain why they don't have it. That might make them look bad and not as spiritual as they are pretending to be.

I don't care about how the world may perceive me; I just want to please God and walk in His blessings. People may think I'm just as carnal as can be, but I don't care. That's their problem. I'm going to walk in the blessings of God.

Set Free From Poverty

As we have already seen, Jesus has redeemed us from the curse of the Law, poverty being a part of that curse. But just as with any provision of God's Covenants, there are certain things we have to do to appropriate the blessings of promise.

This is true concerning salvation. You have to believe in your heart and declare with your mouth that Jesus died for your sins before you can ever be saved. Even though salvation has already been bought and paid for, you have to do something to appropriate that blessing in your own life.

Christ redeemed us from the curse of the Law by taking our place. That's how He did it: through substitution. He broke the sentence of poverty that came upon man through the fall of Adam. That's just a part of what He did, but that's the part we are focusing on in this study. Christ broke the curse, or the sentence, that came upon man after Adam's fall. As a result, we have been set free from the punishment of poverty.

Poverty was a part of what Adam had to endure as a result of his insurrection, or high treason, against God — when he followed the word of the devil. Jesus has set us free from the punishment of poverty, which came into existence with man's sin in the earth. He purchased for us the opportunity to enter back into covenant with God. That's what Jesus has done.

Be Used as a Vessel of Blessing

Though poverty will not keep you out of heaven, there is a good possibility that it will keep other people from going to heaven. They have to hear the Gospel of Jesus Christ being preached in order to receive the Truth and begin a relationship with Almighty God.

But it takes money to preach the Gospel and get the Word out to the world. That's why this message has to be preached in these last days. The harvest that awaits us is going to take a tremendous amount of finances to reap. If you don't have the prosperity to support the work of God that's reaching out to share Jesus Christ with others, that work won't get done.

The question is simply this: Are you willing to care more for the world than you do for yourself? Really caring for the world means you will believe God for prosperity and be a vessel of that financial blessing to help reap the harvest of souls.

It's going to take effort to get enough money so that this work will get done. It's going to take strong, diligent, aggressive, militant faith. People willing to be that way will be tremendous instruments in these last days. We have to drastically change the way we think and believe about certain things.

I believe there is a holy indignation rising among God's people to hate poverty and to see the wealth of the sinner brought into the hands of the just in order that the harvest be gathered. (Prov. 13:22.)

You know for a fact now that Jesus has redeemed you from the curse of poverty. As a result, you can be that vessel used by God to support the preaching of the Gospel to the world in these last days.

3

Delivered From the Religious World

The apostle Paul in writing to the Roman church says:

I beseech you therefore, brethren, by the mercies of God, that ye present your bodies a living sacrifice, holy, acceptable unto God, which is your reasonable service.

And *be not conformed to this world*....

Romans 12:1,2

In sharing this message of prosperity for God's people, I am not trying to be like the world; I have no desire to be like the world. I want us to become like that delightsome land spoken of by Malachi. He said all the world would look at those people and say: "They are blessed. They have something we don't have. The hand of God must be upon them." (Mal. 3:12.)

Changed From the World's Ways

Continuing in Romans 12:2:

And be not conformed to this world: but be ye transformed by the renewing of your mind....

The word *transformed* is from the Greek word meaning "metamorphosis."[1] It's like a caterpillar going through the process of metamorphosis to become a butterfly.

---

[1]Strong, "Greek Dictionary of the New Testament," p. 47, #3339.

We are to go through a complete transformation, or process of change. Spiritually, this process starts when we are born again, but we have to move on from that point. This process affects our soul (or mind, will and emotions), our body, our finances, our family — the entire way we live.

There is to be a complete transformation of our lives. We cannot stay hooked to the world's system. It doesn't matter what the price of gasoline may become; we are not tied to that. We are not tied to the Dow Jones Industrial Index or to prime interest rates. We are tied to an invisible kingdom — the kingdom of God. We are to be transformed from the ways of this world and to be completely revolutionized into the ways of God's kingdom.

How is that going to come to pass — just by hoping and praying? Never. Romans 12:2 says it will come to pass by the renewing of our minds — as our "stinkin' thinkin'" is replaced by the truth of God's Word. We have to change the way we think and the way we look at things. It's this renewing of our mind that will firmly establish us on the road to prosperity.

We change the way we think by starting to think in terms of having a covenant with God. No longer are we strangers or aliens, without hope in this world. We have hope in our God through Jesus Christ. (Eph. 2:12.) We can do all things through Christ Who strengthens us. (Phil. 4:13.)

We may stand in the middle of a need, but we are not standing there with no God. Our God is in and among us, just as He was with Moses at the mouth of the Red Sea. Moses had a rod and he had a God. That same God is with us today.

The same God Who raised Jesus from the dead is telling us that He is going to meet our needs. But we have to change the way we think. We have to renew our minds. Why?

> ...that ye may prove (or establish or know) **what is that good, and acceptable, and perfect, will of God.**
>
> **Romans 12:2**

We are not really going to know God's will without renewing our mind and changing the way we think. How do we renew our mind? The Bible tells us in James, chapter 1, verse 21:

> **...receive with meekness the engrafted word, which is able to save your souls.**

Here is another biblical phrase, *saving the soul*, which is synonymous with *renewing the mind*.

How do we do that? By receiving with a teachable spirit the Word of God.

None of God's people know it all; in fact, most of us know very little. We have to be teachable. We have to prove and establish the will of God in order to experience this change, this metamorphosis, this transformation in our lives. As I said in the introduction to this book, this is going to involve killing some sacred cows.

There is no use in even looking at things about the covenant of prosperity without first talking about being willing to change the way we view God. We have to change our view of prosperity.

God Is Not Religious

I know this is hard for religious people to accept, but "religion" isn't of God.

So many of God's precious people are not prosperous because they have accepted religious lies instead of biblical truths. Religion has worked hard trying to twist and mess up the minds of God's people.

God is not religious. When Jesus walked the earth, He was not religious; in fact, He hated religion. His words and actions were absolutely contrary to the religion of His day. God's people had taken the covenant they had with God and had made a religion out of it. Jesus didn't come so that a new religion could be formed; He came to set the record straight. He came to give us life and to redeem us from destruction.

Today people try to take our relationship with God and make a religion out of it. But it's not a religion; it's walking with God. We are co-laborers, or partners, with God in the earth. We are not to take a partnership and make a religion or ritual out of it. It needs to be something real and vital in our lives.

Traditions of Men

Religious lies, instead of biblical truths, have told people that God doesn't want them to have anything. Jesus put it this way: "The traditions of men make the Word of God of none effect in your life." (Matt. 15:6.)

If it's God's will for His people to be prosperous, why are so many precious believers suffering poverty and lack in their lives? Because of the traditions of men. These traditions of men try to nullify the power of God's Word in their lives.

For instance, there is a tradition that says healing passed away with the apostles. Nowhere in the Bible is God's healing power connected to just the apostles. They themselves said these things came not by their own power or holiness but by the name of Jesus and faith in that Name. (Acts 3:12,16.) Neither will you find in the Word of God that healing has passed away. God still heals today.

Healing is a part of the promises and blessings of God. So is prosperity.

Jesus Stood Against Religion in His Day

Let's look at a situation in Jesus' day when the religious people — the scribes and Pharisees — complained about some things Jesus was doing. These men were experts in theology. Yet they did not know or recognize God as He stood there beside them. Lots of people are like that in the world today.

> **Then came to Jesus scribes and Pharisees, which were of Jerusalem, saying,**
>
> **Why do thy disciples transgress the tradition of the elders? for they wash not their hands when they eat bread.**
>
> **Matthew 15:1,2**

Religion doesn't really care about people and their needs. All it cares about is protecting and maintaining its traditions. These religious people were saying: "We have to preserve our customs, our code, our rules and regulations." That's what religion is all about.

But Jesus didn't have a religious bone in His body. I love what He asked in response to them:

> **Why do ye also transgress the commandment of God by your tradition?**
>
> **Matthew 15:3**

Then He gave them an example by picking one of the Ten Commandments, one of the basics. He didn't have to look too hard. He just said, "Here...let's talk about your traditions."

> **For God commanded, saying, Honour thy father and mother: and, He that curseth father or mother, let him die the death.**
>
> **Matthew 15:4**

33

God's Word simply says we are to honor our parents. It doesn't say we have to honor them just until we are eighteen years old. It says we are to honor them — period!

> **But ye say, Whosoever shall say to his father or his mother, It is a gift, by whatsoever thou mightest be profited by me;**
>
> **And honour not his father or his mother, he shall be free....**
>
> **Matthew 15:5,6**

God had commanded His people that they were to honor their father and mother, taking care of them until their death. But somewhere along the way, they came up with their own tradition. By saying they owed nothing to their mother and father, they could then be released from their responsibilities.

Notice what Jesus said about their tradition:

> **...Thus have ye made the commandment of God of none effect by your tradition.**
>
> **Ye hypocrites....**
>
> **Matthew 15:6,7**

Religious tradition has made the Word of God of none effect. In other words, it has robbed God's Word of its power. We are warned to avoid situations where people are **having a form of godliness, but denying the power thereof** (2 Tim. 3:5).

Religious Traditions Oppose God's Word on Prosperity

As Jesus said, the traditions of men make the Word of God of none effect. Traditional thinking — like the idea that money is the root of all evil — is not the true Word of God. Neither is the idea that rich people can't go to heaven. God's Word doesn't say that! If rich people couldn't go to heaven, then Abraham would be in hell today. When he died and left this world, he left behind a great estate.

Of those who trust in uncertain riches, who put their faith in money and worship it, Jesus said: **How hardly shall they that have riches enter into the kingdom of God!** (Mark 10:23). These people don't know the Word of God, but they know traditions. They have heard the Scriptures twisted.

All the religious traditions God's people have heard through the years have absolutely robbed them from having the Word of God to produce in their lives. They need to get back to the truth of the Scriptures.

The preaching of God's Word concerning prosperity is just like preaching about other subjects. You have to preach salvation until people are saved. You have to preach healing until people are healed. You have to preach the baptism in the Holy Spirit until people are filled with the Holy Ghost with evidence of speaking with other tongues. You have to preach prosperity until God's people begin to experience some wealth in their lives. It's His Word which God watches over to perform in us. (Jer. 1:12.)

God's Word Contradicts Tradition

In Ephesians, chapter 2, we see a description of the way we were before we knew Christ:

> **That at that time ye were without Christ, being aliens from the commonwealth of Israel, and strangers from the covenants of promise....**
>
> **Ephesians 2:12**

This is an important Scripture for us today, especially those of us who were brought up in traditional churches. This Scripture dispels and totally contradicts what many theologians teach: that certain promises are only for the Jews.

I remember sharing with the pastor of our denominational church about a particular promise, dealing specifically with healing.

He said, "But that's just for the Jews."

So I took him to the book of James, chapter 5, which says:

> **Is any sick among you? let him call for the elders of the church; and let them pray over him, anointing him with oil in the name of the Lord** (v. 14).

He responded by saying, "That's just for the Christian Jews who have a right to be healed."

But that's not what *my* Bible says! According to Romans, chapter 10, verse 12, God is rich toward all who call upon Him and there is no difference among us. It specifically says there is no difference between Jew and Gentile in Christ Jesus.

Contrary to religion and tradition and all preconceived ideas about God, about Christians, about preachers and about money, I'm here to tell you, based on the authority of God's Word, that Christians are to be financially prosperous.

4

Obeying Covenant Rules

Let's look now at Ephesians, chapter 2, beginning with verse 10:

> **For we are his workmanship, created in Christ Jesus unto good works, which God hath before ordained** (or prepared) **that we should walk in them.**
>
> **Wherefore** (or because of this) **remember, that ye being in time past Gentiles in the flesh, who are called Uncircumcision by that which is called the Circumcision in the flesh made by hands;**
>
> **That at that time ye were without Christ, being aliens** (or outsiders) **from the commonwealth of Israel, and strangers from** *the covenants of promise,* **having no hope, and without God in the world.**
>
> **Ephesians 2:10-12**

This is a picture of the individual who does not know Jesus Christ as personal Lord and Savior.

But today, as New Testament believers, we have been brought into these **covenants of promise** with God. Notice it says *covenants* **of promise.** That's plural.

God had several different covenants, or contracts, that He had cut with people throughout the Old Testament. He cut one with Abram, renaming him Abraham, and established other covenants with men like Moses, Joshua and David.

Once spoken over the nation of Israel, these covenants were established as everlasting and eternal. God would never change them. He said:

> **My covenant will I not break, nor alter the thing that is gone out of my lips.**
>
> **Psalm 89:34**

After God gave Israel the area which we call the Holy Land, He never changed His mind. It doesn't matter what our government says or what the United Nations may say. It doesn't matter what anybody says. That land belongs to Israel. Why? Because God said so. People can fight over it and debate about it, but that doesn't matter. This land belongs to God's people as the nation of Israel, and they will have it in the end. So it would behoove us to get on their side.

Our Partnership With God Through Jesus

Notice that this Scripture in Ephesians, chapter 2, talks about **the covenants of promise** and how we inherited them. It goes on to say that we were:

> **...strangers from the covenants of promise, having no hope, and without God in the world:**
>
> *But now in Christ Jesus* **ye who sometimes were far off are made nigh by the blood of Christ.**
>
> **Ephesians 2:12,13**

Before Christ Jesus, we were strangers to God and His ways. We had no rights to any kind of relationship with God. But now through Jesus we have begun a relationship, a partnership, with Almighty God, the Creator of heaven and earth.

Beginning then in verse 13, our relationship with God through Jesus is described. It says:

> **But now in Christ Jesus ye who sometimes were far off are made nigh by the blood of Christ.**
>
> **For he is our peace, who hath made both one, and hath broken down the middle wall of partition between us;**
>
> **Having abolished in his flesh the enmity, even the law of commandments contained in ordinances; for to make in himself of twain one new man, so making peace;**
>
> **And that he might reconcile both unto God in one body by the cross, having slain the enmity thereby.**
>
> **Ephesians 2:13-16**

Through the blood of Jesus Christ, we have been brought into covenant with God. Using a more modern-day term, we could say we have entered into a contractual relationship with God.

Our covenant with God is based upon exchange. When two people enter into covenant, all that one has becomes property of the other.

By the blood of Jesus we now have a right to claim every contract, every clause, every promise that God ever made to His people in His Word. If it has been promised in God's Word, no matter who it was promised to, it now belongs to us through Jesus' blood. We have a right to claim each and every promise.

That's why it doesn't matter who God made these promises to. When God made the covenant through Jesus, it was a covenant of promise. By virtue of His blood, we have a right to everything God has ever promised — whether it be healing or prosperity or all the blessings found in Deuteronomy, chapter 28.

This Covenant Comes by Knowing God's Word

I want to point out something right now: The covenant of prosperity requires that the Word of God be given preeminence in your life in order to bring it to pass. You see, you won't receive anything from God outside of His Word. You need to read your contract.

Some people say, "I want you to pray for me." Prayer is great; but getting results takes knowing the Word.

Others say, "I want you to believe God with me for my business." That's fine, and I will, but it's still going to take the Word of God in your heart.

Look at Acts, chapter 20, verse 32:

> **And now, brethren, I commend you (or give you a recommendation) to God, and to the word of his grace, which is able to build you up, and to give you an inheritance among all them which are sanctified.**

Notice what God's Word will do for you. The Word we are studying concerning the covenant of prosperity is going to do two things.

First, the Word will build you up.

Members of the Body of Christ need to be built up. For years people went to church and were beaten down. They left feeling worse than before they came. Now I'm not against any church; I'm just tired of people getting beat up by what they hear from the pulpit.

God's Word will build you up, making you feel like you are somebody. Why? Because you are — in Christ Jesus.

I never will forget when I really got into the Word of God. I began to learn about the word of faith, the word of righteousness, the word of truth. I began to really find out who I was in Christ. That didn't cause pride; it brought a feeling of worth. I learned that I really am worth something to God, that I am God's workmanship, created in Christ Jesus. (Eph. 2:10.)

So, God's Word is able to build you up. Don't feel bad about feeling good when you start seeing yourself in Christ Jesus.

Second, the Word will give you an inheritance among those who are sanctified.

The word *sanctified* means being called out, reserved, washed in the blood of Jesus. This is describing the Church of Jesus Christ.

In this study of the Scriptures regarding prosperity, you may need to find a new and fresh love for these truths. So, get into the Word and allow it to build you up and strengthen your faith.

Maybe you know how to use your faith on little things — and that's fine — but God wants you to move higher. You need to go from having faith for a pair of socks to learning about million-dollar faith and believing for souls to come into God's kingdom. Start believing for things to be added to you that will change lives and bring people into the kingdom.

Don't get me wrong: God wants you to enjoy things. We will be looking at some truths from the Word of God regarding this, because some people feel guilty about having anything in this life. But you need to go beyond just believing for things and start moving to a place of believing for souls. That's big faith!

The Word of God is able to build you up. It will build your faith, but it will deliver unto you your inheritance. You see, it's the Word that makes the difference.

Increase Your Word Level

You might say, "If it's God's will for *everybody* to prosper, how come that person over there isn't prospering?"

Because he has a low Word level in his life.

God's Word doesn't promise that everybody will be a millionaire. It does promise, however, that everybody will have all sufficiency in all things, that they will have the financial freedom and liberty to abound unto every good work. (2 Cor. 9:8.) In other words, they will have all the money they need to do everything God puts in their heart to do, fulfilling the will of God in their lives.

Have you ever had a leading to do something, but just didn't have the money to get it done? Of course, you have. We all have been in that place.

Doesn't it feel wonderful to be able to give financially into a project or a need that arises in your church and see that need met? That's God's will for each of His children. That's what prosperity is.

It is important for you to realize that it's going to take the Word of God for you to experience these things. They don't come just by having some magical desire for them. You have to spend time in God's Word. The Word, by the incorruptible Seed, has the power to bring itself to pass. The human mind cannot fathom how the Word of God works; His Word is absolutely supernatural.

According to Hebrews, chapter 11, you just have to take God's Word by faith. Verse 3 says:

Through faith we understand that the worlds were framed by the word of God, so that things which are seen were not made of things which do appear.

You can't understand this in your head; you have to take it by faith. I just take by faith that all the dirt which we call the earth is made up of something not even visible — the Word of God. The earth was formed by faith.

This rule applies as well to receiving the truth of prosperity in this life. I don't really care what it was made of; I just accept it and receive it by faith. Then I let it come to pass in my life.

Is Financial Prosperity Wrong?

Some people believe it's wrong to pray for "something as carnal as money." It really sets them into orbit when they hear me praying for financial needs.

But it's no more wrong to pray for financial prosperity than it is to pray for joy or peace or forgiveness or healing or any other provision that was bought and paid for by Jesus Christ.

A portion of the prayer Jesus prayed in Matthew 6:11 was, **Give us this day our daily bread.** He was teaching us to pray for our needs to be met. Even though He said, **...for your Father knoweth what things ye have need of, before ye ask him** (v. 8), the Word still tells us that we have to ask. It says, **...ye have not, because ye ask not** (James 4:2).

Philippians 4:19 promises that God meets all of our needs according to His riches in glory. This Scripture is talking about finances. If God has a desire to meet our needs, then we have a biblical right to claim in prayer that those needs are being met by Him.

You may ask, "But doesn't God warn us in His Word about wealth and prosperity?"

Yes, He does. In Proverbs 1:32 He says, **...prosperity of fools shall destroy** (or ruin) **them.** Just don't be a fool. That's simple enough, isn't it?

Follow the Rules

The Word of God warns us about a number of things regarding prosperity. God cautions us about its abuse, about its level of priority in our lives. He also gives us strict admonitions and commandments about what we are to do with money in this life. All we have to do is to obey what He says. Just don't be afraid of it.

As an example, I think of my wife and the attitude she once had toward guns. She and I were on opposite sides when it came to guns. I was brought up in the country in Alabama. If you didn't have a gun by the time you were eight years old, something was wrong with you. My wife, on the other hand, didn't like guns; she was afraid of them.

I took her to a gun class where she was taught gun safety. After going through the class, she began to understand the safety rules concerning firearms. As long as you handle a gun correctly, take precautions and walk according to the rules, then guns are safe.

In the same way, there are safety rules regarding prosperity and wealth. God's Word teaches how you are to keep your heart right concerning prosperity and yet, at the same time, be prosperous in this life.

God wants you to prosper, but He doesn't want you to trust in those riches; He wants you to trust in Him. First Timothy 6:17 says:

> **Charge them that are rich in this world, that they be not highminded, nor trust in uncertain riches, but in the living God, who giveth us richly all things to enjoy.**

You must have the right priorities, recognizing that money is not your source; God is your Source. As long as you keep these things in mind, then you will be safe concerning prosperity and wealth.

Again, you must obey the rules. It's just like driving a car. More people are killed each year in automobile accidents than in airplane crashes; yet many people are afraid to fly. In 1993 alone, 17,449 people died on U.S. highways as a result of drunk drivers.[1] Unfortunately, the U.S. Department of Transportation predicts similar numbers for this year.

Now with this frightening statistic of automobile casualties, did you have any problem driving your car today? Probably not. You just follow the traffic laws, heed the warnings and obey the rules of safety.

That's how you have to view prosperity as well. Yes, it will ruin some people, but only those who do not obey the rules and laws of God which govern it. People who get things out of priority and out of order will always pay the price for it.

But just because some people are doing wrong will not keep me from desiring to have God's blessings in my life. You should feel the same way.

God's Plan for Man Includes Abundance

God's plan from the beginning has always been for His people to experience abundance. Let's go back to the very beginning: the book of Genesis. The word *genesis* means "beginning," so here we find man's beginning. He did not develop from slime out of the sea. He did not evolve over millions of years. He was created by God.

And the Lord God took the man, and put him into the garden of Eden to dress it and to keep it.

Genesis 2:15

---

[1] *1995 Statistical Abstract of the United States.* 115th edition. U.S. Department of Commerce. p. 639.

We find in the creation of man that from the beginning, the very onset of man's existence, God wanted him to have abundance and comfort and success. God planned from the beginning for man to have his every need met, for him to walk in authority, in power, in victory, in success and in prosperity.

God's first man, Adam, experienced no lack. He wasn't just roaming around free as a bird, eating the fruit and acting like some kind of hippie. He had dominion. He was exercising that dominion in a system established by God Almighty. It was not until Satan entered the picture, with Adam's transgression of the law of God, that economic curses and financial hardships came upon mankind.

After Adam's Fall

Notice what happened in Genesis, chapter 3. This is after Adam had transgressed the law of God, after he had disobeyed God's commandment and had eaten of the forbidden fruit:

> And unto Adam he (God) said, Because thou hast hearkened unto the voice of thy wife, and hast eaten of the tree, of which I commanded thee, saying, Thou shalt not eat of it: cursed is the ground for thy sake; in sorrow shalt thou eat of it all the days of thy life;
>
> Thorns also and thistles shall it bring forth to thee; and thou shalt eat the herb of the field;
>
> In the sweat of thy face shalt thou eat bread, till thou return unto the ground; for out of it wast thou taken: for dust thou art, and unto dust shalt thou return.
>
> **Genesis 3:17-19**

After Adam's fall, a result of disobedience to God, financial struggles entered the picture.

Look at verse 14:

> **And the Lord God said unto the serpent,
> Because thou hast done this, thou art cursed above
> all cattle, and above every beast of the field; upon
> thy belly shalt thou go, and dust shalt thou eat all
> the days of thy life.**

Then God began to prophesy, not to this beast, the serpent, but rather to Satan who inhabited and embodied that snake. God was prophetically speaking about Jesus, Who would be born of a virgin. In verse 15 God said:

> **And I will put enmity between thee and the
> woman, and between thy seed and her seed; it (the
> Seed of the woman) shall bruise thy head, and thou
> shalt bruise his heel.**

Jesus Came To Reverse the Curse

Jesus would be sent to reverse the curse that came upon man with Adam's fall. First John 3:8 says Jesus **was manifested, that he might destroy the works of the devil.** A part of these "works of the devil" was financial poverty.

Notice Jesus' words, which He shared in the synagogue at Nazareth on the sabbath. Reading from the book of Isaiah, He said:

> **The Spirit of the Lord is upon me, because he
> hath anointed me to preach the gospel to the poor....**
>
> **Luke 4:18**

Not only had God *anointed* Jesus, but He had *appointed* Him. He had commissioned and commanded Him to preach the Gospel, the Good News, to the poor. And Jesus wasn't talking here about the "poor in spirit." He was talking about preaching the Good News to those who were experiencing financial difficulty, poverty and lack. He was saying, "God has sent Me to preach the Good News to the poor."

What is "good news" to the poor? That they would be redeemed from financial poverty.

He Preached the Year of Jubilee

Jesus goes on to say:

> ...he hath sent me to heal the brokenhearted, to preach deliverance to the captives, and recovering of sight to the blind, to set at liberty them that are bruised,
>
> To preach the acceptable year of the Lord.
>
> Luke 4:18,19

The acceptable year of the Lord means absolutely nothing to Christians of the Western world today. But people who were in covenant with God in Jesus' day knew what He meant when He referred to **the acceptable year of the Lord**. That was a part of the economic plan God had for His covenant people. Every fifty years in the nation of Israel there was to be an extra sabbath, called the year of jubilee. During that year all their debts would be wiped away and their inheritances would be returned to them.

Jesus was saying: "I have come to preach the year of jubilee. This year of jubilee will not just come around every fifty years; it's going to be every day of every year until I return. I have come to set you free from debt."

To the believer, every day is a day of jubilee. You have a right to claim being debt free.

I have had to borrow money in the past, so I know all about that, and I believe it's much more fun to be a lender than a borrower. That's a part of our covenant with God, a part of the blessings of Abraham. It's time for the Church to get bold enough to believe God for that.

Let's not shy away from these things. I want to be like Jesus: fulfilling His Word and experiencing His blessings in my life. I'm satisfied that some of the abuse and extremism in the Body of Christ that was exposed in years gone by was for the sole purpose of scaring the Church back into its little huddle. Some began to think, *Oh, we don't want our people to get too prosperous. It would be better if they are afraid of financial prosperity.*

But Jesus said, "I have come to preach the Good News, the acceptable year of the Lord."

Working as Unto the Lord

Concerning prosperity, Proverbs 10:4 says, **...the hand of the diligent maketh rich.** In other words, diligence brings prosperity or wealth.

But to be prosperous, you have to start working as unto the Lord. If you are serious about prospering, that doesn't mean money will just appear in your mailbox because you happen to watch Christian television. It's going to take some hard work. That's really what separates the men from the boys, or the prosperous from the poor.

You have to learn not just to work hard physically, but to work your covenant with God as well. It takes both.

So if you think you're not going to work, but are just going to use your faith, you need to remember that faith *works.*

According to James 2:20, faith is perfected by our works and corresponding action. I encourage all of God's people to get a job. That's a good place to start. You might say, "But I'm afraid of a job." Well, the Word of God teaches that you should get a job so that you will have money to give.

Learning To Experience Prosperity

There was a time when I dislocated my shoulder and had to wear a brace. Now I realize that during that time I was not in the perfect will of God. I don't mean I was off in some tremendous sin or disobedience to God; it's just that God wanted me well. If I'm not well, I'm not experiencing His best for my life.

The same thing is true concerning our financial lives. When we are not prosperous, when we don't have all sufficiency in all things, we are not living in the perfect will of God. For us to experience that prosperity and please our heavenly Father, we have to do what the Word of God says.

As we have seen in Scripture after Scripture, prosperity opposes any and all aspects of the word *poor*. This does not necessarily mean that every Christian will be living in the highest state of luxury, but it does mean that financial prosperity and abundant supply are God's will for every believer, without respect of persons.

No, not everybody will be a millionaire, but every child of God should have supernatural abundance and financial prosperity in his or her life.

This prosperity will come to pass in your life when you fully open yourself to receive the truth of God's Word and allow His Spirit to work through you as He desires.

5

Activating Your Covenant

I want us to look in the book of Genesis, where God makes a covenant with Abram (or Abraham). We need to remember and remind ourselves that we, as believers today, are in covenant with God through Jesus Christ. He has redeemed us from the curse of the Law. We are joint-heirs with Jesus. Everything He has is ours and everything we have is His.

From the beginning until today, God cut covenants with His people. The word *covenant* means "to cut where blood flows"; in other words, to shed blood, to make a blood contract. Every time God cut a covenant, He entered into a contractual relationship with an individual or a group of people. That covenant always involved an aspect of financial prosperity.

> Now the Lord had said unto Abram, Get thee out of thy country, and from thy kindred, and from thy father's house, unto a land I will shew thee:
>
> And I will make of thee a great nation, and I will bless thee (God is talking about blessing him financially), and make thy name great; and thou shalt be a blessing:
>
> And I will bless them that bless thee, and curse him that curseth thee: and in thee shall all families of the earth be blessed.
>
> Genesis 12:1-3

And Abram went up out of Egypt, he, and his wife, and all that he had, and Lot with him, into the south.

And Abram was very rich in cattle, in silver, and in gold.

Genesis 13:1,2

Every time God cut a covenant with a man, it always included a clause to cover financial prosperity. Why? Because God is a God of prosperity. He wants to prosper those He is in relationship with. As Deuteronomy 8:18 says, **...it is he** (God) **that giveth thee power to get wealth, that he may establish his covenant.**

It takes money to make money. It takes money to preach the Gospel, to get God's Word out to the people and bring them into covenant with Jesus Christ.

God Wants You To Succeed

We have read in Deuteronomy, chapter 28, about the curse of the Law, which begins with verse 15. But in verses 1-14, you will find that part of the *blessing* of the Law was financial prosperity.

God wants you to be a success. He wants you to have a most successful business, a financially prosperous business.

That is a part of the testimony of what Jesus does for people. He doesn't just redeem our souls from hell, though that obviously is the most eternal and most important; He also has redeemed us from the world. He has delivered us out of the authority of darkness and has placed us in a new kingdom, one over which Satan has no control. This kingdom — the kingdom of Almighty God — has a financial plan and an economy all its own.

God's plan is for *every* believer to prosper and to succeed in this life. That's a part of the testimony of what

Jesus Christ will do for you when you turn your whole life over to Him.

Your Covenant With God Includes Prosperity

As a believer today, you have a covenant with God. About that covenant, Jesus says: **Seek ye first the kingdom of God, and his righteousness; and all these things** (like financial blessings, houses, clothes, lands) **shall be added unto you** (Matt. 6:33).

Your covenant of prosperity with God today can be found in the words spoken by Jesus. As He says in Mark 10:29,30, no one will give up anything for the Gospel's sake but that **he shall receive an hundredfold now in this time, houses, and brethren, and sisters, and mothers, and children, and lands....** This hundredfold return won't just come after you get to heaven; it will be now in this life. He continues by saying, **...and in the world to come eternal life.**

In Second Corinthians, chapter 9, we find the perfect plan and will of God for every believer. It describes our covenant with God — the covenant of prosperity.

> **But this I say, He which soweth sparingly shall reap also sparingly; and he which soweth bountifully (or liberally) shall reap also bountifully (or liberally).**
>
> **Every man according as he purposeth in his heart, so let him give; not grudgingly, or of necessity: for God loveth a cheerful giver.**
>
> **God is able to make all grace abound toward you; that ye, always having all sufficiency in all things, may abound to every good work.**
>
> **2 Corinthians 9:6-8**

Verse 8 gives us God's will for His people: that He make all grace abound toward us. Now the word *grace* does not mean some feeling of spiritual goodness. The biblical definition of *grace* is "an impartation of God's power and ability in your life." It is God's power taking over where your ability ends. That is the grace of God.

Some new translations say it another way: how God wants all of the financial blessings and prosperity to be abundantly supplied in your life so that, not only are all your needs met, but you have an abundant supply from which to meet the needs of others.[1] Financial abundance and financial freedom are the will of God for your life. God wants you to be a vessel through which He causes financial prosperity to flow.

When will you know that you are free financially? When you are able to do anything and everything God puts on your heart without always having to look at your checkbook, thinking, *Do I have the money to do the will of God?* God doesn't want money to be keeping you from fulfilling your destiny in Him.

Fulfill Your Obligations to God

You have a covenant with God, but just as with any promise or provision to a covenant, there are things you must do in order to appropriate and activate its blessings. There are contractual obligations you have to fulfill in order to experience this prosperity. There are certain conditions you are required to meet for these things to be activated in your life. It's like any other contract between two individuals: each person must do certain things to fulfill the contract.

Your covenant with God is the same way. God tells you in the New Covenant, or contract, what you must do. Here are some contractual obligations you must follow:

---

[1]Paraphrased from *The Amplified Bible, New Testament*. (La Habra, California: The Lockman Foundation, 1958, 1987).

> **Draw nigh to God, and he will draw nigh to you.**
>
> **James 4:8**

> **Give, and it shall be given unto you....**
>
> **Luke 6:38**

> **All things are possible to him that believeth.**
>
> **Mark 9:23**

There is no such thing as a one-sided covenant, or contract, with God. A covenant is *never* one-sided with God, with Him doing everything for you and you doing nothing for Him. You do your part, then God will do His.

Learn To Work Your Contract

This is an important aspect of your contract with God that you need to understand. God is waiting on you to make the first move and meet the contractual obligations in your contract for prosperity.

This is true regarding salvation: You have to believe in your heart and confess with your mouth. It is true with healing: You have to receive it by faith in God and in His Word. And it is true concerning financial prosperity as well: You have to activate the covenant of prosperity in your life.

What did Jesus do for us? Many people don't really have a clue. When we talk about Jesus redeeming us from poverty and purchasing for us a life of abundance, they don't understand what this really means.

It does not mean that the blessings of God are just going to be automatic in your life. You still have to do something, not to earn them but to activate them. Let me explain what I'm talking about here.

Jesus paid for your right to turn to God, but you have to walk that path. It doesn't just come to you automatically.

God has already forgiven everyone of their trespasses and sins. Now we might know the vilest of sinners, thinking them to be the worst of reprobates; but God is not holding a single thing against them. Yet they could die in their sin and go straight to hell. Why? Doesn't God love them? Yes, He does. Didn't He redeem them and forgive them? Yes, He did. But there is something they have to do: They have to appropriate the redemption that was purchased for them by Jesus.

This is something we all have to do concerning any of the blessings of God. Jesus by His blood has made it possible for us to be in covenant with God. That's what He did for us. But we have to appropriate those blessings by entering into the covenant promises.

According to Ephesians, chapter 2, we were strangers, outsiders. We were without God, without hope in the world. We had no covenant with God. As Gentiles especially, we were on the outside looking in. The blood of Jesus has made it possible for us to be in covenant with God. But that doesn't mean we don't have to work our contract.

You can have a contract in the natural, but that doesn't mean it's going to come to you automatically. You have to exercise the clauses that are written therein. The same thing is true with the Word of God. You have to exercise or work the clauses of His Word.

Delivered Out of the Power of Darkness

There are lots of people who don't really understand their walk with God, because they have never read their contract. They don't know what belongs to them in Christ. That's why they live so far below all of the provisions of God.

If the laws of prosperity are not working for you, it's because you are not working them. The Word of God works. It is infallible. It is incorruptible.

Let's look in Colossians, chapter 1:

> **Giving thanks unto the Father, which hath made us meet (or able) to be partakers of the inheritance of the saints in light:**
>
> **Who (speaking of God) hath delivered us from the power of darkness, and hath translated us into the kingdom of his dear Son.**
>
> **Colossians 1:12,13**

This says God *hath* delivered us from the power of darkness, and *hath* translated us into the kingdom of his dear Son. The word *hath* obviously is past tense. God is not going to do this someday; He has already done it, and He has done it for you as a believer in Jesus Christ.

The word *power* in verse 13 is the Greek word *exousia*, which means "authority, jurisdiction or realm of influence."[2]

God has *already* delivered you from the power (the authority, jurisdiction and realm of influence) of darkness. This "darkness" is referring to the devil, Satan, the destroyer. God has delivered you out of the realm of influence of the destroyer, Satan, who causes poverty.

Translated Into the Kingdom of God

The moment you were born again, you were translated out of the authority of Satan and brought over into a new kingdom — God's kingdom. You are no longer a part of that kingdom of darkness; you are now a part of the kingdom of God. But you have to work the system of the kingdom.

---

[2]Strong, "Greek Dictionary of the New Testament," p. 30, #1849.

Through the blood of Jesus, you have become a citizen of God's kingdom, but that does not mean things are just going to happen for you. You can be a citizen of the United States of America and have all the rights as its citizen, but you have to use those rights. All that you are entitled to won't just come your way automatically.

The same thing is true concerning the kingdom of God. You have been translated out of the authority of darkness, which includes poverty. You have been placed over into the kingdom of God's dear Son, which includes prosperity. But you still have to work God's system.

Get Into the Flow of God's System

God has a system of finance, an economic system, in His kingdom. He neither strays nor turns from that which He has established in His Word.

You have to function within the principles that govern God's economic system in order to activate the promised results of prosperity. Otherwise, you will be like people in the world who don't even have a covenant with God. Though you have a right to that covenant, you won't see the results of it in your life.

Case in point: Consider Joshua. Now Joshua as an Israelite had a covenant with God, part of which involved success and prosperity. But just because Joshua had that covenant with God did not mean he would automatically experience it. He had to get into the flow of God's system.

In Joshua, chapter 1, we see God appearing and speaking to young Joshua as he was taking over leadership after Moses' death. God made a new deal with Joshua as head of the nation of Israel. At one point God said to him:

This book of the law (the Word of God) shall not depart out of thy mouth; but thou shalt meditate

(Hebrew: mutter or speak out loud[3]) **therein day and night, that thou mayest observe to do according to all that is written therein: for then....**

Joshua 1:8

Notice there is a condition. It says you have to meditate (or speak out loud) God's Word day and night. In other words, you have to confess it.

You need to realize that confession and faith and the power of positive speaking were not ideas just thought up by the world; God has always operated these principles. He authored the power of positive speaking when He told Joshua to meditate (or speak and confess) the Word: **This book of the law shall not depart out of thy mouth.** Joshua was a man in covenant with God.

But even though Joshua had a covenant with God, he still had to do something: he had to work God's system in order for God's system to produce in his life. After speaking, or confessing, the Word, Joshua would see the results:

...for then **thou shalt make thy way prosperous,** *and then* **thou shalt have good success.**

Joshua 1:8

Become the Blessed of God

That leads me to another Scripture, Psalm 1. God is a God of success. Aren't you glad? He desires to elevate you to a place of prosperity and success and fulfillment in this life. Psalm 1, verse 1, says:

Blessed is the man that walketh not in the counsel of the ungodly, nor standeth in the way of sinners, nor sitteth in the seat of the scornful.

---

[3]Strong, "Hebrew and Chaldee Dictionary," p. 32, #1897.

Think about it: Who are you listening to and receiving counsel from these days? Don't let it be from the ungodly. That's God's Word on it!

The "scornful" are those who mock or make fun or criticize. Isn't it interesting that it refers to "the seat" of the criticizers? In other words, criticizers are always sitting down. If they would just get up and get active, they wouldn't have time to criticize everybody else.

> **But his delight is in the law of the Lord; and in his law** (or Word) **doth he meditate day and night.**
>
> **Psalm 1:2**

Again, we see that Hebrew word translated *meditate*, meaning to mutter or speak out loud. This person speaks God's Word day and night.

> **And he shall be like a tree planted by the rivers of water, that bringeth forth his fruit in his season; his leaf also shall not wither; and *whatsoever he doeth shall prosper.***
>
> **Psalm 1:3**

You must delight in God's Word, meditating on it and speaking it out loud. Then everything you do, everything you put your hand to, will prosper.

In the world, or the natural, people look at a successful person and say, "That guy just has a Midas touch." I don't want a Midas touch; I want God's touch! Then everything I do, everything I touch, will prosper.

Notice that even though the psalmist David had a tremendous revelation of his covenant with God, he also knew that certain things had to be done in working the system. This is even more true today under our New Covenant with God.

Working the Principles of God's System

Though Jesus has purchased for us the right to walk in covenant with God, we still have to fulfill the contractual obligations, with reference to prosperity. For instance, in Luke 6:38 Jesus says:

Give, and it shall be given unto you....

Now you may say, "But if Jesus redeemed me from poverty and purchased prosperity for me, then it ought to just come to me automatically."

No, He did not purchase a free ride for you. He purchased your right to enter into His kingdom, to come into and function within His system of economy. But you have to work the principles of that system. First, you have to give; then His system will be activated.

Give, and it shall be given unto you; good measure, pressed down, and shaken together, and running over, shall men give into your bosom (or life).

Luke 6:38

6

Seeking the Kingdom

Let's look again in Second Corinthians, chapter 9. Hopefully you will understand even more clearly what the Word of God is talking about here.

> **But this I say, He which soweth sparingly shall reap also sparingly; and he which soweth bountifully shall reap also bountifully.**
>
> **2 Corinthians 9:6**

This verse of Scripture is saying that you, as a believer, have a right to prosperity. But these blessings are not just going to fall on you like ripe cherries off a tree. You have to do something to get them.

Supernatural abundance is a promise of God's Word, but it has to be activated by the believer. Prosperity comes as the result of exercising God's system. If prosperity were like healing, you would not find Second Corinthians 9:6 in the Word of God. But it's there.

Other Scriptures, like Luke 6:38, involve the believer's actions. Again, it says:

> **Give, and it shall be given unto you; good measure, pressed down, and shaken together, and running over, shall men give into your bosom.**

According to this verse, you determine your own measure of financial prosperity by the degree in which you use the laws of the kingdom of God, mainly sowing and reaping. You have a right to prosperity, but you still have to do certain things in order to receive it.

Consider Adam

I want us to look again in the book of Genesis. Adam, in his original state and prior to his sin, was in an obviously intimate relationship with God Almighty. Still, he had to do certain things relative to activating the laws of prosperity.

You know, I think we have some weird ideas about how Adam and Eve lived. We see them just lying around the garden, eating fruit. But this verse of Scripture tells us:

> **And the Lord God took the man, and put him into the garden of Eden to dress it and to keep it.**
>
> **Genesis 2:15**

Adam, the man, had day-to-day things to do relative to taking the resources God had given him and cultivating them, causing them to grow and produce even more.

Here we see Adam before his fall. Though he had many provisions, he was still responsible for operating kingdom laws. I believe those laws were the laws of sowing and reaping. He was placed in the garden to dress it, to keep it, to expand it.

I am convinced from the Scriptures that God gave Adam a particular place called the Garden of Eden. I believe it was a geographical place on this planet given to him by God as a starter seed. Adam was to take that plot of ground and continue planting and reaping, dressing and keeping. Eventually, this whole world would become like the Garden of Eden. That's what his assignment was.

We think of Adam as some kind of prehistoric Tarzan. But he was a manager, a steward. He wasn't here just to play around with the animals. He was given an assignment to subdue the earth.

It's interesting to know the Hebrew meaning for the words *dress* and *keep*. *Dress* means to enslave or to subdue, while *keep* implies protection from enemies by raising a hedge or barrier.[1] Adam was to take the earth back from Satan and to protect it from his influence. Satan's control before Adam was created is obvious to me, considering the dinosaurs and other fierce creatures that once roamed the earth. Science can tell you that this world has gone through a dramatic metamorphosis from what it once was.

Adam was to take the earth and make it paradise after Satan had ruined it, having tried to lead an insurrection against God. Notice that Adam had the protected right to prosper, but it only came by working the plan of God. Man has to do something in the kingdom of God to activate and cause the principles of prosperity to manifest in this life.

Seek After Kingdom Principles

The New Testament was not brought into existence to do away with God's kingdom. Jesus did not come to introduce a new system that would replace God's ways of doing things or change His methods of operation. God did not change those methods with the sacrifice of Jesus. According to Genesis 8:22, there will be sowing and reaping as long as the earth remains. That is a principle in the kingdom of God.

Jesus' death, burial and resurrection absolutely did not change the kingdom. He introduced to us a new and living way whereby we have entrance into the kingdom. (Heb. 10:20.)

Before the Fall, Adam had a healthy body. Through Jesus Christ, we have been restored back to where we have

---

[1]James H. Strong. *New Strong's Exhaustive Concordance of the Bible.* (Iowa Falls, Iowa: World Publishing, 1986), pp. 111,157.

the right of healing, the provision of healing in our covenant with God. We have been given the legal right to function and operate God's system and all of its principles. As legal citizens of God's kingdom, we also have the right to prosper.

Financial prosperity to the believer is a blessing from God. Again, this is the prosperity talked about in Proverbs 10:22, which says, **The blessing of the Lord, it maketh rich, and he addeth no sorrow with it.** This kind of prosperity comes only from God.

There are people who are rich relative to the world's system, but not rich toward God. Being rich toward God is not a geographical issue, relative to either earth or heaven. It has to do with you and the kingdom of God. Your prosperity is based upon your having used the principles of God's Word.

Notice again Matthew 6:33, in which Jesus says:

But seek ye first the kingdom of God, and his righteousness; and all these things shall be added unto you.

Here we see a commandment from the Lord Jesus Himself. In this chapter He has been talking about finances and material things, like houses, clothes and food. A challenge has been issued by Jesus to believers relative to divine prosperity in their lives.

Have the Desire To Accomplish

Prosperity today is a protected right that comes as a result of doing two things: discovering how God's kingdom works, then working the kingdom. Notice Jesus said that we are to seek first the kingdom. That means finding out how God's kingdom works.

In order to prosper in any system of economy, you have to know how it works. God's kingdom is no different. If you want to experience supernatural abundance of prosperity in your life, you have to seek first the kingdom of God — find out how God's kingdom works — and then work it.

If you want all things to be added unto you, don't feel like a heel or like some less-than-spiritual Christian because you have set financial goals in your life. The Lord created us with some ambition and motivation. It seems, however, that some believers have let the devil steal from them.

God has placed within us a desire to accomplish. We have been made in the image of God. We are to be creative and build things. God is a builder, and we are to be builders, too. The apostle Paul called himself a masterbuilder, who was building the kingdom of God. (1 Cor. 3:10.) We have to discover how the kingdom of God works.

That's what Jesus was talking about in Matthew 6:33. He was saying, "If you seek first the kingdom and His righteousness, all the things you have need of will come to you."

Some people may read that Scripture and say: "Don't worry about working. Just go to church and make sure you have a relationship with God. Then somehow mystically He will just get those things to you."

But that's not what verse 33 says. You have to discover how the kingdom of God works, but you also have to learn about His righteousness.

Understanding Righteousness

People have some warped ideas about righteousness. *Righteousness* is a broad word in Scripture. It has to do with your right standing with God, your relationship with Him, your being purchased by the blood of Jesus and having your sins wiped away. But these are just parts of the word *righteousness*, just as with salvation.

Salvation doesn't only mean being born again. It is an all-inclusive word that deals with every aspect of your life, including spirit, soul, body, financial and social.

Verse 33 is not saying, "You just go to church and get saved, then God will make sure you have all these things." It says you have to find out about the kingdom of God and His righteousness. You have to seek out the kingdom and learn how it works.

In James, chapter 2, righteousness is seen as a life of hearing and obeying the Word of the Lord. Let me explain. Verse 21 tells about how God told Abraham to go to Mount Moriah and offer his son, Isaac, as a sacrifice on the altar. So Abraham took his son up that mountain, laid him at the altar and was about to sacrifice him to God. Verse 23 refers specifically to how Abraham **believed God, and it was imputed** (or counted) **unto him for righteousness.** Abraham was really living a life of obedience. He heard and then obeyed. When you obey God, you are living in righteousness.

God Blesses the Obedient

Again, seeking first the kingdom of God and His righteousness is a twofold operation: first, you discover how the kingdom of God works; and, second, you live that life of obedience — hearing from God and doing what He says to do.

We have already talked about how the rules of prosperity work in the kingdom: by sowing and reaping, planting and harvesting.

You have to learn those principles and then do what God says. When He moves on your heart to do something, you must obey. God blesses the obedient. As Isaiah 1:19 says:

If ye be willing and obedient, ye shall eat the good of the land.

You have to develop a lifestyle of hearing and obeying God. By using the principles of sowing and reaping, of hearing and obeying, you will see prosperity produced in your life.

That's what happened in the life of Abraham. We could put it this way: Abraham believed God, listened to God and obeyed God's instructions. Like the psalmist says:

The steps of a good man are ordered by the Lord: and he delighteth in his way.

Psalm 37:23

As you listen, hear and obey God, He will lead you in a procession of victory upon victory. The result will be a life of prosperity with you having all sufficiency in all things. Through that prosperity you will be able to support the kingdom of God. That's what Jesus is talking about.

Maybe you need a breakthrough in your finances. This study will help you to understand the fact that part of your breakthrough in finances has to begin on the inside of you.

As we have read in Matthew, chapter 6, Jesus is talking about finances and prosperity. Again, in verse 33 He says, **Seek ye first the kingdom of God, and his righteousness; and all these things shall be added unto you.** He is talking here about having abundance and a supernatural supply, about God taking care of you financially.

He is saying: "You have to discover the operation of My kingdom. Learn how to apply its principles in specific areas of your life. Work the principles and laws of My kingdom and obey My instructions. Then all these things will be added unto you. While other people are always sweating and worrying and fretting over how to receive things in their lives, My blessings will be added unto you because you are working My system of economy."

7

Working Kingdom Principles

I want us to take a little side trip here that may help you, especially if you have been attending church for a long time. Maybe you're one of those veterans of religion who are like concrete — thoroughly mixed up and too well set!

You might say, "But I've heard all these arguments about prosperity before."

I want you to realize that as we are studying God's Word about prosperity, we are looking at both the Old Testament and the New Testament, both the Old Covenant and the New. You need to understand some things about the Old and the New Covenants, or contracts.

In Matthew 5:17 Jesus said:

> **Think not that I am come to destroy the law, or the prophets: I am not come to destroy, but to fulfil.**

One morning before church, I was in prayer, putting some final touches on these thoughts I have been sharing in this study. I had meditated on these Scriptures for years. Then the Holy Spirit began to give me some tremendous insight concerning the relationship between the Old and the New Testaments. It seems that religion has robbed God's people of some powerful blessings that were written under the Old Covenant.

The New Testament — the New Covenant or new contract, that which we have through faith in Jesus Christ

— was not brought into existence to do away with God's method of operation. The New Testament was introduced to give us a different way of entering into God's kingdom and His system of operation.

When you start talking about things like tithes or sacrifice, people will say, "Oh, that's *Old* Covenant." No, tithes and sacrifice have nothing to do with the Old Covenant, or the Law. They have nothing to do with either the Old or the New Covenant; they have to do with the kingdom of God.

Our Legal Right to Kingdom Principles

You see, the New Testament was not established to do away with God's system of economy, but to give you an easier way to enter into it and get involved with it. You don't get to God through the blood of goats and bulls; you get there through faith in the blood of Jesus Christ.

In the New Covenant we have been given, as Hebrews 10:20 says, **a new and living way**, whereby we have access to God the Father through Jesus. We have the legal right as citizens of God's kingdom to function in it.

Israel had functioned in God's system of economy by promise, not by legal right. They had not been born again; they were still children of the devil in that they had not been spiritually changed. They only operated in God's kingdom by promise.

We operate in it by legal right as citizens of the kingdom of God. God didn't change His kingdom or alter His system of operation. All He changed was the way we enter into that kingdom, giving us the right of citizenship to function therein.

Becoming skillful in the covenant of prosperity, or learning how to appropriate the provisions of financial prosperity, really is simpler than most people try to make it.

Learning how to appropriate the purchased provision of financial prosperity is simply becoming skillful in the way God's kingdom operates. In other words, activating God's promise of prosperity comes as you discover the way God's economy works and then work it. God's kingdom principles bring blessings in your life when they become a reality to you. That's what Jesus was talking about in Matthew, chapter 6.

It's just like anything else, even in the natural. Once you have learned how to work the plan, the plan will always work.

Are You Serving God — or Money?

Lots of people can't stand hearing preachers talk about money. Maybe you don't like it, either. If so, you would have had a real problem with Jesus. Study the gospels, and you will find that approximately twenty of His messages deal with money and/or stewardship over natural resources, specifically that of money or lands or possessions.

Jesus preached often about money. In Matthew 6, verse 21, He says:

> **For where your treasure is, there will your heart be also.**

In other words, if you want to find the reality of where your heart is in anything, all you have to do is to look at your checkbook ledger. See where you spend your time, where you spend your money. That's where your heart really is.

Jesus is trying to teach people that they can't serve God and money. (Matt. 6:24.) He wants us to understand that, though we cannot serve God and money, we can serve God *with* our money. Then by serving God, we will be able to appropriate the financial blessings He desires us to have.

The Pursuit of Things

People are constantly being caught up in the pursuit of things. But Jesus says we are not to be that way. Notice His words in Matthew 6, verse 31:

> **Therefore take no thought, saying, What shall we eat? or, What shall we drink? or, Wherewithal shall we be clothed?**

In other words, He is saying: "Don't get caught up in the cares of this life. That would be seeking the wrong things. Get your eyes off of the product."

Here is the problem: By spending all of your time pursuing the product, you will not be involved in the process that produces it.

In Matthew 6:32 He says:

> **(For after all these things do the Gentiles seek:) for your heavenly Father knoweth that ye have need of all these things.**

God knows you have need of all these things and He wants you to have them.

Focus on the Process

Then Jesus tells us in verse 33:

> **But seek ye first the kingdom of God, and his righteousness; and all these things shall be added unto you.**

You need to focus on how the kingdom of God works. If you will discover the kingdom, focus on how it works and then work its system, those things will automatically come into your life. You won't have to be out pursuing them, because you are focusing in on what produces them, on what activates them. Matthew 6:33 is asking you to focus on the process, not the product. When you focus on the process, the product will be manifested.

As a kid, I loved to look at those muscle-building guys. Obviously I focused on the product and not the process. That's what many people do; they dream about the product, thinking, *Oh, wouldn't that be good?*

Jesus is saying: "Work My kingdom. Seek first the kingdom of God and your walk with Me. Put Me first. Learn how My kingdom operates. Then all these other things will be added to you."

In Matthew 6:33 Jesus is not preaching in terms of receiving reward for being good; He is speaking in terms of the fruit or result of your doing what the kingdom of God says — using the Word of God.

Sowing and Reaping

How does God's kingdom work? It works simply on the basis of sowing and reaping.

In Genesis, chapter 8, God is speaking, not only naturally but financially and spiritually as well, especially concerning His kingdom. In verse 22 He says:

While the earth remaineth, seedtime and harvest, and cold and heat, and summer and winter, and day and night shall not cease.

In other words, as long as the earth exists, there shall always be seedtime and harvest. If you want to flow in the kingdom of God on this earth, you will have to operate in these principles of sowing and reaping.

Many people know about sowing and reaping only in terms of the religion they have been taught. They have heard it like this: "You reap what you sow. If you do bad, you will reap bad." That is a small part of it. It governs not just a holy lifestyle, but everything in your life.

Let's look now in Mark's gospel, chapter 4. Jesus is saying this is active in the kingdom of God, even today.

> **So is the kingdom of God** (or this is how God's kingdom works), **as if a man should cast seed into the ground;**
>
> **And should sleep, and rise night and day, and the seed should spring and grow up, he knoweth not how...**
>
> **And he said, Whereunto shall we liken the kingdom of God? or with what comparison shall we compare it?**
>
> **It is like a grain of mustard seed, which, when it is sown in the earth, is less than all the seeds that be in the earth:**
>
> **But when it is sown, it groweth up, and becometh greater than all herbs, and shooteth out great branches; so that the fowls of the air may lodge under the shadow of it.**
>
> **Mark 4:26,27,30-32**

The kingdom of God works like seedtime and harvest, like sowing and reaping. This truth is neither Old Testament nor New Testament; it is God's system of economy. He is the Lord our God, Who changes not. (Mal. 3:6.)

God's system of seedtime and harvest, of sowing and reaping, has been in operation from the very beginning, and it shall be to the very end. Planting and reaping is the most basic law of God. It works in every area of your life and it certainly governs the laws of financial prosperity.

Giving and Receiving

Now, I want to point out something from the tenth chapter of Mark's gospel. In chapter 4, Jesus was talking about it in terms of sowing and reaping. In chapter 10, He is teaching about giving and receiving. All these principles

— sowing and reaping, giving and receiving — are a part of God's economy.

> **And Jesus answered and said, Verily I say unto you, There is no man that hath left house, or brethren, or sisters, or father, or mother, or wife, or children, or lands, for my sake, and the gospel's.**
>
> **Mark 10:29**

Notice He is not just talking about giving up a relationship. There are times of giving financial resources and houses and lands. I know what it is to give away a house and property; I have done it. I have given away expensive things, but never remorsefully. Though I have read verse 29, I also have read verse 30! It says:

> **But he shall receive an hundredfold now in this time....**

When will I receive this blessing — when I die and go to heaven? No. It says, **...now in this time**. I gave that money and those things because I wanted to obey God. But I also gave it because my mama didn't raise a dummy! Jesus said, "If you give, you shall receive a hundredfold now in this time."

You might say, "Well, brother, you're going to get back some good feelings for giving it."

Then let's read on:

> **But he shall receive an hundredfold now in this time, houses, and brethren, and sisters, and mothers, and children, and lands....**
>
> **Mark 10:30**

You can receive a hundredfold return on your giving! When you give up property for the kingdom of God, you can receive a hundredfold of that property now in this time.

But notice what goes with it. Verse 30 says: **...with persecutions....**

When you're poor, nobody hates you or envies you or is jealous of you. When you're driving around in that old clunker that's held together with bailing wire, nobody will criticize you. But start looking more prosperous and you'll be told about all those people who are starving in Africa. Your being poor isn't going to help those people one bit, but being blessed will.

Notice the kingdom of God works on sowing and reaping, on giving and receiving. But it doesn't just work on the principle of "give and immediately receive." Don't wait to receive before you give again. You have to keep on giving.

It's like the farmer: he sows and he reaps; then he takes from that which he has reaped and sows it again; then he will reap even more. That crop continues to grow bigger and bigger.

The same is true financially. When you give out, it is given back unto you. Then you take from that which you have received and give out some more. You build through God's principles of sowing and reaping.

Wealth To Establish God's Covenant

Now let's look at a verse of Scripture from Deuteronomy, chapter 8. Verse 18 says:

> **But thou shalt remember the Lord thy God: for it is he that giveth thee power to get wealth, that he may establish his covenant which he sware unto thy fathers, as it is this day.**

God wants His people to be wealthy for the establishment of His Covenant.

This Scripture says that God gives us *power* to obtain wealth, but I have no idea why it was translated that way.

The Hebrew word for *power* actually means "wealth."[1] With the more literal rendering of that word, this Scripture is saying, "God gives you wealth to obtain wealth."

God gives you a seed to sow. He is giving you something to give out. He gives seed to the sower and then multiplies the seed that is sown. Many of the things in your life right now were brought to you by God, not as an actual provision for you, but as that which you are to give away by sowing into the kingdom. This, then, will provide for you a greater harvest.

Too many people are eating their seed when they should be sowing it. As it is given out, it will bring in the harvest.

The Right *to* Prosperity

The covenant we have entered into through the blood of Jesus is not a right *of* prosperity, but rather a right *to* prosperity. There is a big difference. This is where so many people get confused about prosperity. They get frustrated and end up getting mad at God.

Let me explain the difference between the right *of* something and the right *to* something. The right *of* something means you are entitled to it as a benefit. The right *to* something means you are given the opportunity to receive it; you have the authority to pursue a certain thing under the protection and guidance of a higher authority.

An example of having the right *of* something would be to receive healing as one of the benefits you have the right to receive. In the beginning, Adam was created perfect; his body was perfect and he was perfectly well. As a believer in Jesus Christ, you have been redeemed back to that original place, where you too can have the right of healing, the right of health.

---

[1] Strong, "Hebrew and Chaldee Dictionary," p. 55, #3581.

In the United States, one of the rights provided for every citizen is freedom of speech. That means you have the liberty to say whatever you want to say. Now you may get yourself into trouble because of the words you choose to say, but you still have the freedom to do so.

Let's contrast that freedom of speech with the right to bear arms. This right to bear arms does not mean you will automatically receive the benefit of a firearm. But you have the right to pursue the obtaining of that weapon under the guidance and protection of a higher authority.

Prosperity works the same way.

It's important for us to make a contrast between prosperity and mere provision. You have a right to provision. God is going to take care of your basic needs; He has promised that. Jesus said the birds don't sow or reap or toil, yet God provides for them. (Matt. 6:26.) Mere provision to exist is built into your covenant with God. You have a right to that.

But prosperity means more than just barely getting by; it's supernatural abundance. That's where many people don't make the proper distinction, rightly dividing the Word of Truth. (2 Tim. 2:15.) There is a difference between mere provision and supernatural abundance.

You have a right *to* prosperity. Through your covenant with God, you are entitled to the opportunity for it. You have been given the authority to pursue prosperity under the guidance and protection of God's Word and in submission to the authority of the Lord Jesus Christ.

This is the difference between healing as a benefit and prosperity as a purchased right to pursue.

Again, to receive healing, you don't have to do anything outside of believing and then receiving. Of course, there are things that can hinder your healing, like unforgiveness or a lack of faith.

In Psalm 103 healing is called one of the "benefits of the Lord," but supernatural abundance (financial wealth) is not listed as one of these benefits in that psalm. However, "satisfying your mouth with good things" (v. 5) is included, and that certainly would indicate or imply that your basic needs would be met.

But I am talking about more than just provision. I am talking about prosperity, about the wealth of the sinner being laid up for the just. (Prov. 13:22.) This is the financial inversion God's Word talks about in the last days, for the purpose of reaching this world for Jesus Christ.

Again, here is the difference: In your covenant with God, you don't have the right *of* prosperity; you have the right *to* prosperity. The difference is that with the right *to* prosperity you still have to do certain things. As you work the kingdom principles set out in your covenant with God, you will see prosperity being manifested in your life.

8

Dethroning Money as Your Lord

In this study on our covenant of prosperity, we have already seen from the Word of God that financial prosperity is God's will and desire for every believer. In all actuality, financial prosperity is a part of our redemption in Christ Jesus. Jesus bought and paid for us to have a prosperous life.

As we have noted in our study, the curse of the Law was a curse that came upon the Israelites in their disobedience. Yet that curse had its origin way back at the fall of man, with Adam's transgression.

A part of the curse that came upon Adam, as well as the curse specifically listed in Deuteronomy 28, included an aspect of poverty. It is the eternal struggle of individuals to always be working so hard; yet no matter how hard they work, they never have enough to experience financial freedom and blessings in this life.

It's important for us to define prosperity in God's terms. True prosperity is having all sufficiency in all things and abounding unto every good work.

God wants your family blessed. How did we ever buy into the religious lie that God doesn't want us to be blessed financially, as if money were dirty?

You know, we have developed some weird ideas about money. We call it "cold, hard cash." But it's soft and warm. We have bought into all of the lies that religion has said about money.

Think about God being toward us the way a loving parent is with his child. We want our kids to be dressed well, to experience comfort, to be happy. God is even more loving than you and I ever will be.

We have been redeemed from a life of poverty and have been brought into a place where God wants to prosper us.

Every time God cut a covenant, entering into a relationship with an individual or a people, it always had a provision and a promise of abundant supply. That's because, contrary to what many people think, God is rich. Do you realize that? I'm not just talking from a standpoint of heaven with streets of gold and a throne filled with jewels; I'm talking about God being rich in this earth. It belongs to God. As Psalm 24:1 says:

> **The earth is the Lord's, and the fulness thereof.**

In the book of Haggai we read:

> **The silver is mine, and the gold is mine, saith the Lord of hosts.**
>
> **Haggai 2:8**

God has all the money in the world, all the resources in the world. He owns this earth. He is rich, not only from heaven's standpoint, but in this natural, physical realm. A covenant is based upon exchange.

The reason we as believers have a right to claim financial abundance is because everything God has is ours. I'm a joint-heir with Jesus Christ, so that means it's mine, too! I have a right to claim it. I have a right to stand upon the promises of God's Word concerning prosperity.

Contrary to religion and tradition and all preconceived ideas about God and Christians and preachers and money and wealth, I'm here to tell you based on the authority of God's Word that Christians are to be financially prosperous.

You Can't Serve God and Money

One of the greatest breakthroughs and one of the most important areas of freedom that believers can experience is found in Matthew, chapter 6, verse 24. Jesus says:

No man can serve two masters: for either he will hate the one, and love the other; or else he will hold to the one, and despise the other. Ye cannot serve God and mammon.

Today many Christians are allowing money to lord it over them. They need to dethrone money in their lives.

Money should not be your lord; that is the place only Jesus can fill.

You have to be the one to make that declaration, to stand up and say, "Money doesn't tell me what to do; I tell money what to do." I know that sounds bold, and some people may go nuts when you say it. But we are not talking about things in the natural realm; we are talking about things in the kingdom of God.

The Bible says that the carnal (or natural) man cannot receive the things of God; in fact, it says the things of God are foolishness to the natural mind. (1 Cor. 2:14.) Our natural thinking is based on the world's system, which is diametrically opposed to God.

It is important, then, to make sure that money is dethroned in your life. Again I say, money can't be given the lordship over your life; only Jesus can fill that place. But you have to be the one to declare it. How do you do that? By controlling your finances, instead of allowing them to control you.

You have to say: "Money, you don't tell me what to do — I tell you what to do. You're not telling me I can't give in this offering. I'm putting you in the offering plate (or bucket) right now, because God told me to!"

Abraham Dethroned the Natural

When God told Abraham to go and offer his son as a sacrifice, all he said was, "Saddle up, Isaac. We're going up the mountain to offer a sacrifice to God."

Abraham's natural mind must have been arguing with him, saying something like this: "But Isaac is the only kid you've got, Abraham. You were old when he came along and you're even older now. You can't start over again. If you sacrifice your son, how are you ever going to be the father of many nations? Look at this thing logically, Abraham — you're the father of one, and now you're talking about giving him away."

But Abraham dethroned the natural and believed God, allowing the supernatural to be placed on the throne of his life.

Money Isn't Your Source

As we read in Matthew 6:24, Jesus said you cannot serve God and money. Let's get out of our religious thinking for a moment.

Jesus is not just dealing with priorities, or those things we treat as most important.

In verse 24 He is also talking about perspective: how we see, what we see and Who we see as the most powerful in our lives, as our Source and Supply. That's what He wants people to focus in on.

God is your Source, not money.

God is your Supply, not your job.

But in our religious thinking, we say to ourselves: *If I can't serve God and money, that means God doesn't want me to have money and serve Him at the same time. So I've got to be poor to serve God.*

That's a lie of the devil to keep people from being born again and serving God, to keep young men and women from going into the ministry.

See God as the Source of Your Supply

Jesus wants to get across to us a proper perspective of how we see, what we see and Who we see as the most powerful in our lives. Notice He says in Matthew 6:21:

For where your treasure is, there will your heart be also.

Then He starts talking about the eye or, in other words, how you perceive things. He says in verse 22:

The light of the body is the eye....

Your life will be determined by the way you look at things.

If you see money as the source of your happiness, and trust in it for success in your life, you will be filled with darkness. The devil will lead you around like a bull with a ring in its nose.

You have to look to God, with your eyes focused on Him as the Source of your supply. Then your eyes will be filled with light.

Jesus is teaching people to trust in God as their Source, not in the world's system. This is not the only place Jesus dealt with this issue.

The Rich Young Ruler

In Mark, chapter 10, Jesus tries to get this principle across to the rich young ruler. Not only was this young man religious, he was righteous by the religious standards of his day, but he was also a wealthy individual.

He comes to Jesus and asks, "What can I do to inherit eternal life?"

Jesus says to him, "Keep God's Word and do all the commandments."

He answers, "I already do those."

> **Then Jesus beholding him loved him, and said unto him, One thing thou lackest: go thy way, sell whatsoever thou hast, and give to the poor, and thou shalt have treasure in heaven: and come, take up the cross, and follow me.**
>
> **Mark 10:21**

Jesus wanted this young man to make a sacrifice, to experience a lifestyle change and go to a higher level. He came to Jesus in the first place because he was not satisfied with where he was, not only in his walk with God but in his covenant of blessings. He had reached a comfortable plateau. But that was not where he wanted to be in God.

He was asking Jesus: "What can I do to obtain that abundant life, that supernatural life You talk about? What can I do to enter into this next level of supernatural living with the power of God?"

Jesus said in response to him, "This is what I want you to do: obey Me — do what I say."

But he couldn't do that. He was unable to get out of his little rut of just sowing seeds as he purposed in his heart. He wasn't able to enter into that lifestyle of sacrifice. As a result, he missed out on a blessing. The Scripture says:

> And he was sad at that saying, and went away grieved: for he had great possessions.
>
> Mark 10:22

Don't Trust in Riches!

> And Jesus looked round about, and saith unto his disciples, How hardly shall they that have riches enter into the kingdom of God!
>
> Mark 10:23

It really bothered people for Jesus to say this; in fact, verse 24 says:

> And the disciples were astonished at his words....

They were surprised at Jesus' words. Why? Because this was so contrary to what He had preached. He had always preached a gospel of good news to the poor. Then all of a sudden He makes this statement: **How hardly shall they that have riches enter into the kingdom of God!** (v. 23).

Let's read on in verse 24:

> ...But Jesus answereth again, and saith unto them, Children, how hard it is for them that trust in riches to enter into the kingdom of God!

He wasn't talking about heaven here. He was talking about God's economic system of sowing and reaping.

If people have faith just in the balance of their checkbook ledger, instead of in God's kingdom principles, how will they ever enter into God's system of giving? How are they going to walk in supernatural giving if they only have faith in what they can see, feel and hear?

Lots of people say, "If I was wealthy, I would be giving into the kingdom of God." I'm not so sure they would.

Others who are living in abundance say, "I can't give right now. I've got this big deal coming up and I need to hold on to my money for that." People get caught up trusting in those "big deals."

Just remember: those "deals" are not your Lord.

Many people claim to be Christian businessmen with Jesus as their Partner. But it's a funny thing how, as their business partner, Jesus has absolutely no checkwriting privileges.

Jesus said:

> ...how hard is it for them that trust in riches to enter into the kingdom of God!
>
> It is easier for a camel to go through the eye of a needle, than for a rich man to enter into the kingdom of God.
>
> Mark 10:24,25

Remember, "the rich man" is the one who trusts in money as his source and supply. It's easier for a camel to go through the eye of a needle than for that man to enter into God's kingdom.

"The kingdom of God" Jesus refers to here is not heaven. He is talking about entering into God's system of sowing and reaping.

Again, I point out how important it is for us to dethrone money in our lives.

In First Timothy, chapter 6, Paul is talking about these same things. Concerning those who are wealthy in this world's goods, he says:

> Charge them that are rich in this world, that they be not highminded, nor trust in uncertain riches, but in the living God, who giveth us richly all things to enjoy (v. 17).

There are some traditions about money that people need to dispel from their minds. It seems the Bible gets misquoted regarding this subject. People are always saying, "The Bible says, 'Money is the root of all evil.'" But that's not what the Bible says. Money is neither evil nor good; it has absolutely no virtues or vices. The thing that matters about money is what we do with it.

Paul also writes:

> **For we brought nothing into this world, and it is certain we can carry nothing out.**
>
> **And having food and raiment let us be therewith content.**
>
> **1 Timothy 6:7,8**

The word *content*, or *contentment*, here does not mean a form of satisfaction that is free from ambition or that which is associated with mediocrity, apathy or the absence of goals. In this instance, the word *content* expresses the thought of thankfulness, appreciation and gratitude.[1] God wants you to have a life of thankfulness.

Some people need a breakthrough in just learning to be thankful for what they have. In fact, they won't be receiving more from God until they are thankful. Prosperity is a stewardship issue.

Paul goes on to say:

> **But they that will be rich fall into temptation and a snare, and into many foolish and hurtful lusts, which drown men in destruction and perdition.**
>
> **For the love of money is the root of all evil....**
>
> **1 Timothy 6:9,10**

---

[1]Vine, W. E. *Vine's Expository Dictionary of Old and New Testament Words*. (Grand Rapids, Michigan: World Publishing, 1981), p. 234.

This is why you have to keep your heart right and be sure that money is dethroned from its place of influence in your life. Money should never be telling you what to do. Any time you feel that money is becoming a big priority in your life, you need to start giving. Write a big fat check and drop it in the offering basket. That will cure your flesh!

Again, verse 10 says:

For the *love* of money is the root of all evil....

It's the love of money, not the possession of it, that is the root of all evil. There are people without a nickel in their pocket who are in love with money.

For the love of money is the root of all evil: which while some coveted after, they have erred from the faith, and pierced themselves through with many sorrows.

But thou, O man of God, flee these things; and follow after righteousness, godliness, faith, love, patience, meekness.

1 Timothy 6:10,11

Maybe you need a financial breakthrough in your life. In order to experience financial abundance based upon biblical principles, you have to take money down off its throne in your life and let God have complete control. You have to always make sure that it's God telling you what to do with your money, not your money telling you what to do with God.

9
Moving to a Higher Plane

Though you have the promise of divine prosperity, you have to do something for it to be activated in your life. As we have learned, you have to work the principles of God's kingdom as you operate within His system of economy.

There are two aspects to working God's system of economy. People get confused by not realizing this.

First, there is the natural or human side — the physical realm. Then there is the spiritual or divine side — the realm of the Spirit. One without the other will produce only a limited amount of God's blessings in your life.

The Natural Side

Let's take, for example, the natural side. God's Word advocates a strong work ethic. It does not promote the use of a welfare system. It says simply if you don't work you don't eat. (2 Thess. 3:10.)

There will always be people who are unable to take care of themselves. It is our responsibility to care for them, and we should do that. But these people are different from those who refuse to see after their own needs, always expecting to be cared for by others.

You see, God's system of economy teaches diligence. Don't get mad at the guy who worked harder than you. If you want the kind of things he has, then go to work. It's just that simple. This is the natural side. Certainly the natural side alone will bring a certain amount of God's blessings.

The Spiritual Side

Then there is the spiritual side — when you plant the seed of God's Word in your heart and release your faith.

Many people don't realize there are even two kinds of seeds. Money is the physical seed; God's Word is the spiritual seed. By planting the physical seed of your tithes and offerings, you will see a certain amount of blessings in your life. But if you don't also plant spiritual seed through God's Word, you will never have the faith to reap the harvest promised by His Word.

There are always these two sides to the situation: the natural and the spiritual. Again, one without the other will produce a certain level of prosperity; but, when properly combined, they always produce supernatural abundance. That is the focus of our study at this point.

Be a Cheerful Giver

Let's consider the combination of both sides, relative to planting. You can be planting the Word in your heart, or confessing with your mouth, or learning to release your faith, or sowing financial seeds, or working the principles of diligence. All these actions really boil down to the use of sowing and reaping. You will reap what you sow. This is a foundational principle and truth in the Word of God.

> **But this I say, He which soweth sparingly shall reap also sparingly; and he which soweth bountifully shall reap also bountifully.**

> **Every man according as he purposeth in his heart, so let him give; not grudgingly, or of necessity: for God loveth a cheerful giver.**

> **2 Corinthians 9:6,7**

Verse 7 says you are not to give grudgingly. Don't get upset every time an offering is taken in a church service. You need to get glad, thinking, *This is another opportunity for me to get blessed.* Then you can be a cheerful giver.

> **And God is able to make all grace abound toward you; that ye, always having all sufficiency in all things, may abound to every good work.**
>
> **2 Corinthians 9:8**

When you are that cheerful giver of verse 7, then as verse 8 says, God is able to make this grace — this supernatural ability to prosper — abound toward you, so that you have all sufficiency in all things and may abound unto every good work.

> **As it is written, He hath dispersed abroad; he hath given to the poor: his righteousness remaineth for ever.**
>
> **2 Corinthians 9:9**

Notice how this word *righteousness* is in context with being obedient in your giving.

God's System of Economy

> **Now he that ministereth seed to the sower both minister bread for your food, and multiply your seed sown, and increase the fruits of your righteousness.**
>
> **2 Corinthians 9:10**

In this portion of Scripture, there are four aspects, relative to operating God's system of economy, that will set into motion the kingdom principles of prosperity in your life. They are:

- Ministering seed to the sower.
- Ministering bread for your food.
- Multiplying your seed sown.

• Increasing the fruits of your righteousness.

First of all, though not mentioned in this passage of Scripture, there is one aspect of God's system of economy that deserves discussion: the principle of tithing. Let's consider it first.

Tithing

Your tithe is God's. You are not to make an offering until you have paid your tithes. You do not *give* your tithes, you *pay* them.

Tithing is just like being in partnership with another person. Remember, that's what a covenant is, a partnership. You are in partnership with God.

Let's say you and another person are partners, with certain items being jointly owned by the partnership. If you go out and sell one of those items, you are required to give your partner his share. When the money is received from that sale, you are obligated to pay your partner. You are not just giving an offering to your partner; you are paying that which is already his as part owner of the item sold.

In the same way, your tithe is God's; it is *already* His. You are paying Him His part by honoring Him with that tithe. In truth, all that you earn belongs to Him; but He has given you the opportunity to take the other ninety percent and be blessed with it.

Then, beyond the tithe, we have these four aspects of God's system of economy as found in Second Corinthians 9:10. Let's look at each of them.

• Ministering Seed to the Sower

God gives seeds to the sower. As you become really serious about prosperity, God will give you seeds for you to sow — not only seeds of money, but of time and opportunity. He will bring certain things into your life that you are not to consume upon yourself. He will give you those things for you to invest so they can multiply.

At times, God may send a certain thing your way, fully expecting you to hold it for a while, then pass it on. From time to time, He has had me do that.

I never will forget being given an expensive watch. I didn't wear it, because I knew that God had given me that watch so that I would hold it for a while. I kept it, not so I could enjoy it for myself, but so that I could pass it on when God instructed me to do so. In a matter of months He put it on my heart to sell the watch and give the proceeds. As a result, I was able to help a family in our church to pay their taxes and to get out of debt. I was obedient to sow into the kingdom of God.

• Minister Bread for Your Food

From this we see that God brings things into our lives for the specific purpose of taking care of our needs. He wants all of our basic, immediate needs to be met.

The psalmist said:

> **I have been young, and now am old; yet have I not seen the righteous forsaken, nor his seed begging bread.**
>
> **Psalm 37:25**

As God's righteous one, your bills will be paid, so you can release your faith in this promise of God's Word.

• Multiply Your Seed Sown

We find here that God then multiplies the seeds you have sown. He not only gives you the seed to provide for your needs, but He begins to multiply the seeds that are sown.

Notice the seeds that are being multiplied. They are not seeds that you *intended to sow*. They are not seeds that you *thought about sowing*. They are not seeds that you *meant to sow but ate for bread.* God multiplies those seeds that you have actually sown.

- **Increase the Fruits of Your Righteousness**

    I used to read Second Corinthians 9:10 this way:

    > God ministers seed to the sower by ministering bread for food, multiplying the seed you sow and *making you a better Christian.*

    But that's not what it says.

    This fourth level is the breakthrough or level of supernatural abundance referred to as "an increase in the fruits of your righteousness." Remember, righteousness is a life of obedience — listening to God and obeying what He says to do. That's how it was with Abraham: he heard God and obeyed Him.

    It's interesting that the Greek word translated *increase* means to grow; also, to enlarge, according to *Vine's Expository Dictionary.*[1] God will enlarge your fruit. The word *fruit* can mean the effect or actions of your obedience to Him.[2]

    So God will do four things: give you seeds to sow, provide bread for your food, multiply the seeds you have sown and then bring the increase.

Progressive Levels in God's Prosperity Plan

As I was meditating upon this, the Lord said, "These are progressive levels of operating within My system."

It's almost like playing a video game. In this kind of game, you start out on level one and progress to higher levels, receiving entertainment and joy as you progress.

---

[1]Vine, p. 254.
[2]Ibid., pp. 133,134.

Just as there are levels in a video game, there are also levels in God's prosperity plan.

When people know about sowing seeds, they operate at that level of prosperity. As they progress to the next level, they enjoy a certain amount of blessing. By progressing, they are not only sowing seeds but actually seeing what they sow being manifested back in their lives. An absolute direct result of their giving is the income they are receiving. They have made it to level two!

Then with level three, not only do they see their needs being affected because of what they are giving, but they actually begin to see themselves getting ahead as God is multiplying the seeds they have sown. They have reached level three in God's system of economy.

This seems to be where most sincere, dedicated Christians stop. They reach a plateau, thinking they are on top, when all the time God has an even higher level.

Supernatural Abundance

We have discussed in this study how Abraham obeyed God and it was imputed unto him for righteousness. Because of his obedience to God, he learned that God is Jehovah-jireh, the Lord Who meets our needs. At that point, he went from level three to level four, thinking, *No matter what situation I'm in, God is more than enough!*

Abraham abounded in prosperity to the point that he taught his son, Isaac, about it.

In Genesis, chapter 26, Isaac was in a particular land where there was famine. He had a plan to leave, but God interrupted that plan and said to him:

> **Go not down into Egypt; dwell in the land which I shall tell thee of:**

> **Sojourn in this land, and I will be with thee, and will bless thee....**
>
> **Then Isaac sowed in that land, and received in the same year an hundredfold: and the Lord blessed him.**
>
> Genesis 26:2,3,12

As a result of his obedience, Isaac was able to experience hundredfold returns on every investment he made. Why? Because he learned about that fourth level of prosperity.

Not only did Isaac sow seeds, but he made a sacrifice. What was the sacrifice he made? Doing what God wanted, not what he wanted. He sacrificed his own will, putting it in submission to God's will. That's what brings breakthrough.

Second Corinthians 9:10 says, **...and increase the fruits of your righteousness.** This word *increase* can be translated from the Greek as "enlarge."[3] God wants to enlarge your harvest. Could you use an enlargement, financially speaking?

God brings enlargement or growth. How? By the results of your obedience to make sacrifices for the kingdom of God. That enlargement is the result of your obedience.

The Importance of Sacrifice

In this study we have considered to some extent the operations of seedtime and harvest, sowing and reaping, giving and receiving, planting and gathering.

There are specific words involving the first half of these operations: seedtime, sowing, giving and planting.

---

[3]*New Strong's*, p. 19.

One word we have discussed in our study is *obedience*.

Another word we need to consider in our understanding of God's economic system is the word *sacrifice*. Most people don't really know what it means.

The word *sacrifice* is the offering of anything to God in worship; the giving up or foregoing of something valuable for the sake of gaining something of greater value.

You may say, "That sounds like investment."

That's exactly what sacrifice is. It's looking beyond today and seeing tomorrow. It's planting into the kingdom of God by faith, believing that it will come back unto you good measure, pressed down, shaken together and running over.

Sowing Seed Vs. Sacrifice

Let's show the biblical difference between sowing a seed and making a sacrifice. They are totally different.

A sacrifice is always a seed; it is the planting of that seed into the kingdom of God. But a seed isn't necessarily a sacrifice. A seed is that which you determine in your heart. **Every man according as he purposeth in his heart, so let him give** (2 Cor. 9:7).

Here is another analogy: A rich man has money, but a man with money isn't necessarily rich.

Sowing seeds will take you all the way to level three in the blessings of God, but it takes sacrifice to move you on to level four. Let me explain.

Sacrifice doesn't mean killing an animal; it means the offering of anything to God in worship. More specifically, it means the giving up of something valuable for the sake of something of greater value. According to *Vine's Expository Dictionary of New Testament Words*, a sacrifice is not only the act of offering to God, but it is also that which is offered, like material or financial things.[4]

Sacrifice is the giving of something that brings within you an immediate lifestyle change. In other words, you feel the difference when you make a sacrifice. You can sow a seed without it affecting your lifestyle at all, but you can't make a sacrifice without it costing you something, without it producing a lifestyle change.

Contrasting between seeds and sacrifice, a sacrifice is that which is given by the bidding of the Lord. In Second Corinthians 9:6,7 a seed is that which you give voluntarily. Notice it says: **He which soweth sparingly shall reap also sparingly; and he which soweth bountifully shall reap also bountifully. Every man according as he purposeth in his heart....**

This is the law or principle that governs the sowing of seeds. You determine it. You say, "I'm going to plant a seed here." You make the decision to do it and you determine the amount. Sowing seeds is based upon your own will.

Again, making a sacrifice is that which is given by the bidding of the Lord; it is based upon obedience, requiring the absolute submission of your will or plans to the will of God.

A sacrifice is that which God asks you to do. It is the Holy Spirit speaking upon your heart to give up something. Jesus was preaching about this in Mark, chapter 10. No one has ever given up anything when asked by God to do it, but that he has received **an hundredfold now in this time...and in the world to come eternal life** (v. 30).

God multiplies the seeds that you sow, but He brings enlargement or growth through sacrifice. **The fruits of**

---

[4]Vine, p. 313.

your righteousness mean the results of your obedience to do what God says with your money. Again, a sacrifice is that which is given by the bidding of the Lord, and it is based upon obedience.

Sacrifice Brings Prosperity

This is where great prosperity lies. Not just in tithes and offerings. Not just in the sowing of seeds. But in the increase of the fruits of your righteousness, as you hear and do what God says with what you have, like Abraham did.

The devil has tried hard for years to keep this truth hidden from the Church.

As we have seen, Abraham's obedience brought provision and abundance into his life. He planted seeds and operated in kingdom principles. Then God spoke and told him to go and make a sacrifice. God was saying to him, "I want you to do this for Me. I want you to give this up for Me."

That's what sacrifice means. It doesn't mean to draw blood or to kill. It means to offer up something valuable and precious to God, like time, for instance.

Abraham took Isaac up on that mountain, because he was willing to do it. He was hearing and obeying God. He lifted that knife in obedience to God and was about to bring it down when the Lord stopped his hand. Immediately he was shown a ram in the thicket that was to be offered in Isaac's place as a sacrifice.

In Abraham's act of hearing and obeying God, God was declared as Jehovah-jireh, the Lord Who provides — Who hears and sees and meets our needs. (Gen. 22:14.)

Are you asking, "Where is Jehovah-jireh in my life?" You need to be living in the fruits of righteousness, so that the Holy Ghost can be moving upon your heart to do things. As God's Word says, if you are willing and obedient, you will eat the good of the land. (Isa. 1:19.)

10

Breaking Through
Into Supernatural Abundance

We have taken much time and effort in this study to examine Scripture after Scripture proving that it is God's will for you to prosper financially.

As a believer in Jesus Christ, you have been brought into the covenants of promise by the offering of His blood. One of those covenants of promise is the covenant of prosperity. As a part of the New Testament, prosperity is yours. You have the legal right to it.

You have certain rights and privileges as a citizen of the kingdom of God; yet, within those rights and privileges, you have to function within God's system of economy and operate the laws of His kingdom.

Now, in studying about covenant, we have learned what a covenant is and its relationship to the kingdom of God. So many people have the wrong idea about the New Testament, or New Covenant, thinking it does away with the Old. But as we have learned, the New Testament was not brought into existence to do away with the Old. Nor was it introduced to change God's system or His methods of operation.

God did not change when Jesus died on the cross. As He said through the prophet Malachi, **I am the Lord, I**

change not (Mal. 3:6). So Jesus' death, burial and resurrection did not change God. Its purpose was to introduce a change in our lives as believers.

The New Testament, or New Covenant, was brought into existence to introduce a new and living way, whereby we might have entrance into the kingdom of God. We can enter boldly, not by the blood of goats and bulls but by the blood of Jesus Christ.

Israel could not enter into the kingdom of God as legal citizens; but its people operated under covenant in God's kingdom, in His system, in His methods and ways. Though they would at times experience the supernatural, they only operated there by promise.

By believing in Jesus, you can operate there today with legal rights as a citizen of His kingdom. You are a part of the family of God by the blood of Jesus Christ. As a result, you are allowed to function within God's system of operation or His economy.

The sad thing is that the children of this world, the children of darkness, are more efficient in operating their kingdom than believers are in operating theirs. This is why we need to learn more about how to operate in the kingdom of God.

Dividing Covenant and Kingdom

It is important that you rightly discern the truth regarding covenant and kingdom. Through a covenant you enter into relationship with God, but God's kingdom remains the same. This is why you cannot throw out the Old Testament altogether.

Within the Old Testament, God reveals how His kingdom works. As we learned in Joshua 1:8, God's kingdom works by believing and speaking His Word. Also, Proverbs 18:21 tells us that life and death are in the power of the tongue. Isaiah 55:9 describes how God's ways are higher than our ways. God has an entirely different level of operating, but He is telling us, "I have sent My Word so that you can know how to function within My kingdom."

So you can't just throw out the Old Testament as passe', for within it are revealed so many truths of how God's kingdom operates.

It is important, then, to divide between covenant and kingdom. Your covenant with God has to do with the way you enter into relationship with Him. The kingdom of God existed before that covenant was enacted. His kingdom has been established since the beginning of time and will always be.

Obedience Brings Results

As we have learned in our study, sowing seeds is something you determine to do. Making a sacrifice is something you do in obedience to God. Again, Jesus said:

> **Seek ye first the kingdom of God, and his righteousness; and all these things shall be added unto you.**
>
> **Matthew 6:33**

First, you have to seek to know how God's kingdom operates — in sowing and reaping — but also you have to live a life of obedience to God. Being obedient is doing what God says for you to do, when He says to do it, where and how He says to do it.

This obedience brings results. As Jesus says in verse 33, **...and all these things shall be added unto you.** The "things" He is referring to are your physical needs being met. As we learned previously about Abraham and Isaac, they were obedient to God and, as a result, physical things were added unto them.

Let's look again in Mark's gospel, chapter 10. Notice Jesus' words in verses 29 and 30:

> **Verily I say unto you, There is no man that hath left house, or brethren, or sisters, or father, or mother, or wife, or children, or lands, for my sake, and the gospel's,**
>
> **But he shall receive an hundredfold now in this time....**

Jesus is teaching about a lifestyle change. He is saying in this verse: "Nobody has ever given up anything for the Gospel — not just sowing a seed, but giving up something God whispers by His Holy Spirit in your heart for you to do — without receiving a return from God."

Anyone who makes this kind of sacrifice to God will receive from Him a return for it: he can receive **an hundredfold now in this time**.

God's system of economy involves breaking over into supernatural abundance. This supernatural breakthrough doesn't come from just sowing a seed as you purpose it in your heart. It's more than just having your basic needs met. It's not just seeing an increase on what you have sown. This breakthrough comes as you obey God, doing things in the natural that may seem ridiculous or even impossible.

As Jesus said, we are to seek first the kingdom by operating in those kingdom principles and living in His righteousness. This aspect of righteousness involves enlarging the results of your righteousness in God, or your obedience to Him.

Peter Sacrificed His Own Will and Plan

Let's consider a passage from Luke, chapter 5:

> **And it came to pass, that, as the people pressed upon him to hear the word of God, he stood by the lake of Gennesaret (the Sea of Galilee),**

> **And saw two ships standing by the lake: but the fishermen were gone out of them, and were washing their nets.**
>
> **And he entered into one of the ships, which was Simon's (or Peter's), and prayed him that he would thrust out a little from the land. And he sat down, and taught the people out of the ship.**
>
> **Now when he had left speaking, he said unto Simon, Launch out into the deep, and let down your nets for a draught.**
>
> **And Simon answering said unto him, Master, we have toiled all the night, and have taken nothing....**
>
> **Luke 5:1-5**

In other words, in verse 5 Simon Peter was saying, "Jesus, I've tried that already."

If I only had a nickel for every time someone has told me that! They say things like, "I've already tried that healing business" (or that faith business or that soul-winning business). My response to them is: "Obviously you didn't do it the way God said."

You need to keep on doing what God says to do. God's Word doesn't say, "Be a *trier* of the Word." It says, "Be a *doer* of the Word and you'll be blessed in your deeds." (James 1:22,25.)

So Peter says, "Jesus, we've already tried that." But, thank God, Peter didn't stop there. He said:

> **Master, we have toiled all the night, and have taken nothing: *nevertheless at thy word* I will let down the net.**
>
> **Luke 5:5**

Here we see Peter's righteousness, his obedience to God. Peter had a will and a plan. He had probably been thinking, *I've worked all night with no results. I'm tired, so I'm going home to get some food and some rest.* That was *his* plan.

But Jesus had a different plan. He said to Peter, "I want you to submit to this." So Peter submitted, sacrificing his own will and submitting his own plan to the will and plan of God. He said to Jesus: **...nevertheless at thy word I will let down the net.**

Peter's Obedience Brought Supernatural Abundance

This was the result of Peter's obedience:

> **And when they had this done, they inclosed a great multitude of fishes: and their net brake.**
>
> **Luke 5:6**

That was quite a catch! They didn't just bring in enough to get by; they came up with more than they could handle! They were obedient, doing what Jesus said to do.

> **And they beckoned unto their partners, which were in the other ship, that they should come and help them. And they came, and filled both the ships, so that they began to sink.**
>
> **Luke 5:7**

This is an example of supernatural breakthrough to abundance. The key to Peter's breakthrough was his response to Jesus: **...nevertheless at thy word I will let down the net.** He was saying, "It's not what I want, but what You want, God. You tell me what to do, and I'll do it."

You Can Experience It Too!

You, too, can experience this lifestyle of breakthrough, this supernatural abundance. It appeared in the lives of Old Testament patriarchs and New Testament followers of

Jesus Christ as seen in the book of Acts. But to experience it, you have to do what they did to get it.

They did more than just sow a seed, more than just believe God for their needs to be met, more than just believe Him for their increase. They lived a life of righteousness and obedience to God. As a result of their obedience — of doing what God said to do, when He said to do it, how and where He said to do it — God enlarged them.

This principle separates mere provision from supernatural prosperity.

The Secret To Entering Abundance

Jesus teaches about this in John, chapter 12. People seem to read religiously the things Jesus said, yet they don't understand all He is talking about. In this chapter, He gives us the secret of entering into abundance in the kingdom of God. In verse 24 He says:

> **Verily, verily, I say unto you, Except a corn of wheat fall into the ground and die....**

He is speaking prophetically of His own life, but this is also a principle that governs God's kingdom: **Except a corn of wheat fall into the ground and die....** He is obviously speaking of a lifestyle change. We are to die to self by dying to our own will and submitting it to God's will.

Again, Jesus says in verse 24:

> **Except a corn of wheat fall into the ground and die, it abideth alone: but if it die, it bringeth forth much fruit.**

Supernatural abundance comes when you die to self, when you die to your own will and your own plans.

We all have plans for our lives. Everything we have has come from the Lord, but we seem to be making our own plans, like what we will do with our nest egg, for instance. We need to submit those plans to God.

When we seek His desire and His will concerning what to do, and then are obedient to Him, we will see the results He intends: We will bear much fruit. The results of our obedience will bring an enlargement in our lives.

Every major successful Christian businessperson is always sharing with others the key to increasing the fruits of their righteousness. This key is obedience. Obeying God's direction is the single greatest ingredient to financial success. Paying tithes, giving offerings and sowing seeds are basic to this lifestyle of obedience.

Following God

Let's look at another Scripture from the book of Isaiah:

> **Thus saith the Lord, thy Redeemer, the Holy One of Israel; I am the Lord thy God which teacheth thee to profit (or prosper), which leadeth thee by the way that thou shouldest go.**
>
> **Isaiah 48:17**

Obeying the direction of the Holy Spirit is one of the most important aspects for breakthrough into supernatural prosperity. Notice God says: **I am the Lord thy God which** *teacheth* **thee...(and)...which** *leadeth* **thee**. This cannot work if you won't follow God.

Following God is simply obeying, simply doing what God says to do. Following Him is making a sacrifice.

Jesus made the ultimate sacrifice and prefaced it with this prayer to the Father: **...not my will, but thine, be done** (Luke 22:42). In other words, He was saying, "It's not what I want, Father, but what You want Me to do."

I never will forget the prayer I prayed when answering the call to the ministry. I must have prayed it every day: "Lord, You've got me today, but I'm giving You all my tomorrows. My future is Yours. I'll do what You tell me to do. I'll go where You tell me to go. I'll be what You want me to be." The best decision I ever made was to submit my will to His.

Now don't get me wrong: this old fleshly tabernacle — my natural will, desires and plans — will, from time to time, rise up and try to revolt against that agreement. Why? Because, just as with everybody else, my flesh will try to interfere.

It is vital that you keep your life in submission to God and follow His instructions. That means not just in spiritual things, but with regard to financial prosperity as well.

As Jesus said, no man has given up anything for the Gospel's sake [which is sacrifice!] but that he can receive a hundredfold in this life. Breakthrough comes when you follow God, when you obey what God has said for you to do.

In our church, many people have made tremendous sacrifices into our capital stewardship ministry. They have given up things that were valuable and precious to them for something more valuable and more precious: the advancement of the kingdom of God. As a result, they have shared some marvelous testimonies about having experienced supernatural breakthroughs. One particular brother testified how God paid off his house in two weeks. He heard from God and then obeyed. That's supernatural breakthrough!

How will that work for me?

First of all, you have to be willing to listen to God. This is where many people draw the line. They will listen to God about certain things and say, "Okay. I'll work in the nursery...I'll do this...I'll do that." But when it comes to giving money, they close their ears. They certainly don't want to hear what God has to say about that!

A Blessing or a Curse?

Let's use an analogy about how something God would intend to be a blessing to His people can, through neglect or abuse, become a curse. God gave the Israelites the ark of the covenant as a way for them to have absolute victory in their lives. On the other hand, if they didn't use it in the right way, a curse could come against them.

Under Moses' leadership, the Israelites were given the ark in order to signify God's presence in their lives. It symbolized God on the throne as the real king of their nation. The ark was placed within the Holy of Holies, draped with a covering so no man could see it or touch it, and the focus of the people was turned toward that place of worship.

The ark brought tremendous victory in their lives. When it was carried on poles out into the battlefield, as God had instructed, a glory went forth from it, annihilating the enemy.

The ark had been given by God with specific instructions about its care and use. When the Israelites obeyed God's instructions, the ark became a way to activate victory and supernatural abundance in their lives.

However, by ignoring God's direction concerning the ark, the very thing God had intended to be a blessing for them became a curse. This happened while David and his army transported the ark back to the tabernacle.

Along the way, David had not been careful to use the ark as God had intended. He did not obey God's direction concerning its transportation. As a result, while the ark was being carried on the back of an ox cart, Uzzah reached to steady it and, when he touched it, fell dead. (2 Sam. 6:6,7.)

It was through disobedience and negligence to God's instruction that the very thing God had intended as a blessing brought about a curse in their lives.

Finances are the same way. Your tithe, your offering, your obedience concerning sacrifice are things God intends for you to do in order to receive blessings in your life. But if you, like Israel, don't do as God says to do by following His directions, they can be like a curse.

The tithe is probably one of the touchiest aspects in people's lives, yet it's the very thing God put into motion to bring a blessing. As we have read in Malachi, chapter 3, it brought a curse to the nation of Israel, because they abused it.

There are certain things God intends as blessings in your life today. But you can run from those things. You can deny them, neglect them, ignore them. That means the very thing God intended as a blessing in your life can become a curse — if you don't use it in the right way by being obedient to God's instructions.

Be Radical in Your Obedience to God

I want to encourage you to step over into this other level that will bring enlargement to you as a result of your obedience to God. It comes by hearing Him and obeying Him.

Again, Isaiah 48:17 says:

> **Thus saith the Lord, thy Redeemer, the Holy One of Israel; I am the Lord thy God which teacheth thee to profit, which leadeth thee by the way that thou shouldest go.**

This won't work if you don't follow God's instructions. It won't be manifested if you won't do what God has said to do. You really have to be radical about this kind of obedience to God.

My friend, it takes the consistent and accurate work of sowing seeds, believing God for your needs to be met, believing Him to multiply the seeds you have sown, and then receiving an enlargement as the result of doing what God has said to do.

Many times God has told me, "Give this away...Give that away." When He does, I am obedient. I give it away — whether money or things — not because I'm such a spiritual person, but because I know about Mark 10:30. I never make that kind of sacrifice, being obedient to God by giving up something valuable and precious, without it coming back to me in a hundredfold measure.

I believe there are some tremendous principles we all need to activate in our lives. You see, God does not ask the question, "What do you want to receive?" He asks, "What are you going to do with what you have right now?" That kind of obedience will cause your needs to be fulfilled.

An Example of Obedience Through Sacrifice

We have learned in this study how God brings enlargement or growth and increase as the result of your obedience through sacrifice.

Again, sacrifice is more than sowing a seed. That seed, or offering, many times is based upon your own decision as you purpose in your heart to give. Your sacrifice is made based upon obedience to the Lord as He has spoken to your heart. This requires the submission of your own will to the will of God. It is giving up something valuable and precious for something more valuable and more precious. It is based upon what God asks you to do.

In First Kings, chapter 17, there is a story of the prophet Elijah going into the house of a widow woman. There is no doubt that this widow was impoverished, having much financial difficulty in her life. Beginning in verse 8, it says:

> And the word of the Lord came unto him, saying,
>
> Arise, get thee to Zarephath, which belongeth to Zidon, and dwell there: behold, I have commanded a widow woman there to sustain thee.
>
> So he arose and went to Zarephath. And when he came to the gate of the city, behold, the widow woman was there gathering of sticks: and he called to her, and said, Fetch me, I pray thee, a little water in a vessel, that I may drink.
>
> 1 Kings 17:8-10

This doesn't seem too serious, but you have to remember there was a drought in the land. It hadn't rained for three and one-half years at that time.

Let's continue in verse 11:

> And as she was going to fetch it, he called to her, and said, Bring me, I pray thee, a morsel of bread in thine hand.
>
> And she said, As the Lord thy God liveth, I have not a cake, but an handful of meal in a barrel, and a little oil in a cruse: and, behold, I am gathering two sticks, that I may go in and dress it for me and my son, that we may eat it, and die.
>
> And Elijah said unto her, Fear not; go and do as thou hast said: but make me thereof a little cake first, and bring it unto me, and after make for thee and for thy son.
>
> For thus saith the Lord God of Israel, The barrel of meal shall not waste, neither shall the cruse of oil fail, until the day that the Lord sendeth rain upon the earth.

> **And she went and did according to the saying of Elijah: and she, and he, and her house, did eat many days.**
>
> **And the barrel of meal wasted not, neither did the cruse of oil fail, according to the word of the Lord, which he spake by Elijah.**
>
> **1 Kings 17:11-16**

I want you to see this woman's act of obedience, the sacrifice that she made. This wasn't something she purposed in her heart. She didn't look at her barrel of meal and say, "This is really getting low, so I need to sow a seed to meet my need." It wasn't a seed she was sowing but a sacrifice she was making.

God, through the prophet Elijah, asked her to give up this that was a part of her family. It was going to produce a temporary lifestyle change in her household. Elijah was saying to her: "If you will do this for me first — if you will give this up for the sustaining of the work of the Lord — as the Lord God lives, you will be supernaturally supplied."

Her Obedience Brought Abundant Supply

The key to this whole passage is found in verse 15:

> **And she went and did according to the saying of Elijah.**

In other words, she acted on the Word of God that came to her through this prophet.

Notice verse 16:

> **The barrel of meal wasted not, neither did the cruse of oil fail, according to the word of the Lord, which he spake by Elijah.**

That's supernatural abundance — a tremendous breakthrough in her finances! She was down to one last meal; but she obeyed God, and He brought an enlargement as the result of her sacrifice. Notice, too, that she was supernaturally sustained from then on.

That Kind of Obedience Will Bring Financial Breakthrough

If we, as God's people, could just get hold of the importance of obeying God in our finances: doing what God says to do, when He says to do it, the way He says to do it. That obedience will bring a financial breakthrough in our lives.

As we saw in Luke, chapter 5, when Jesus told Simon Peter to launch out into the deep, Peter looked beyond his own understanding. When he obeyed Jesus, those nets were filled to overflowing! Peter had a supernatural breakthrough, because he obeyed God and submitted his will to the will of the Lord.

True and genuine sacrifice will bring about a temporary lifestyle change, but it is the secret to breakthrough into supernatural abundance. This, my friend, is what separates mere provisions from divine prosperity. Anyone implying that God doesn't or hasn't led him in sacrifice is really saying God doesn't want him to have a breakthrough in his finances.

If you will pray and really seek God about these things, He will begin to lead you. As we read in Isaiah 48:17, the Lord said He would teach you how to prosper and lead you in the way you should go. But this involves more than just sowing seeds; it involves acts of obedience in sacrifice to the Lord. We have seen this obedience through sacrifice as done by Isaac, by Peter and, of course, by that little widow woman in First Kings 17.

Now many people will say, "I've tried all that, but it didn't help; it didn't work for me."

If these kingdom principles are not working for you, there is a reason. You need to ask yourself some specific questions. We will look at them in this last chapter.

11

Consider Your Ways Before God

In Haggai, chapter 1, it says:

> **Is it time for you, O ye, to dwell in your ceiled houses, and this house lie waste?**
>
> **Now therefore thus saith the Lord of hosts;** *Consider your ways.*
>
> **Ye have sown much, and bring in little; ye eat, but ye have not enough; ye drink, but ye are not filled with drink; ye clothe you, but there is none warm; and he that earneth wages earneth wages to put it into a bag with holes.**
>
> **Haggai 1:4-6**

In our modern-day language, we would say it this way: "No matter how much I make, it's never enough." In response to that, verse 7 again says:

> **Thus saith the Lord of hosts;** *Consider your ways.*

The Word of God is saying that we are to consider our ways — to examine what is going on in our lives and what we are doing (or not doing) in relation to the kingdom of God. Again, God is saying, **Consider your ways.**

Psalm 84:11 says, **...no good thing will he (the Lord) withhold from them that walk uprightly.** God does not withhold good things.

It's interesting to note God's words to Solomon in Second Chronicles, chapter 7. In verse 14 He says:

If my people, which are called by my name, shall humble themselves, and pray, and seek my face, and turn from their wicked ways; then will I hear from heaven, and will forgive their sin, and will heal their land.

In other words, the burden of change is upon God's people.

If this covenant of prosperity is not being activated in your life, you are not to blame God or doubt His promise or discredit His Word. You have to consider your own ways.

Here are some questions to ask yourself relative to the blessings of God coming into your life through divine prosperity, or supernatural abundance.

1. *Are You Being Faithful in the Lord's Tithe?*

In Malachi, chapter 3, verse 8, God asks His people this question: **Will a man rob God?** Then He says to them, **Yet ye have robbed me.** Their response to Him is, **Wherein have we robbed thee?** God's answer is simple: **In tithes and offerings.**

He goes on in verse 9 by saying to them:

Ye are cursed with a curse: for ye have robbed me, even this whole nation.

This curse came upon the finances of Israel because the people had failed to tithe.

Some might say, "But we're under the New Covenant; we're redeemed from the curse."

My response to them is Galatians 6:7, which says:

Be not deceived; God is not mocked: for whatsoever a man soweth, that shall he also reap.

If a person sows, or fails to sow, he will reap one of two things in his life: a harvest or a crop of corruption.

Someone may say, "I'm redeemed from the curse, so it doesn't matter what I do." But it does matter. You must be standing on the Word, activating your covenant with God by working the laws of love under the New Covenant through the blood of Jesus Christ.

As God said in Malachi 3:9, **Ye are cursed with a curse: for ye have robbed me.** The cure to this curse is found in verse 10:

> **Bring ye all the tithes into the storehouse, that there may be meat in mine house, and prove me now herewith, saith the Lord of hosts, if I will not open you the windows of heaven, and pour you out a blessing, that there shall not be room enough to receive it.**

Until you are really and truly faithful with your tithe, you are cutting off all the blessings of God in your life.

Jesus said in Luke 16:12:

> **If ye have not been faithful in that which is another man's, who shall give you that which is your own?**

In other words, if you can't be trusted with what belongs to another person, how can God entrust you with what is yours?

As we learned earlier in this study, the tithe is the Lord's. You are to be faithful with that which is God's, making sure it is brought into the local church. If you don't do that, God is saying, "How am I going to trust you with something that I give you for your own?"

So don't be deceived, thinking that tithing isn't important. It certainly is important in the kingdom of God today.

2. *Are You Taking Care of the House of the Lord?*

We read previously from the book of Haggai, chapter 1. This is dealing with a priority issue. The children of Israel had neglected the construction of the house of God. God was saying to them, "I want a temple, a place where My people can come and worship Me."

Under the New Covenant, the temple of God is not made of bricks and mortar but of men and women, boys and girls — believers. The house of God today is the Church of Jesus Christ. (2 Cor. 6:16.) But God needs and uses buildings and facilities to get His Gospel out and to minister to the people.

In Haggai, chapter 1, God is talking about the physical construction of the kingdom of God. In verse 4 He asks this question: **Is it time for you, O ye, to dwell in your ceiled houses, and this house lie waste?**

Then He says to them: "Do you want to know why prosperity is not working in your life? Consider your own ways. You are not taking care of the construction programs regarding My house. You take care of My house, and I will take care of yours."

In verse 8 He commands them:

> **Go up to the mountain, and bring wood, and build the house; and I will take pleasure in it, and I will be glorified, saith the Lord.**

So you need to consider another question: If prosperity isn't being activated in your life, are you properly taking care of the physical house of God?

3. *Have You Been Faithful To Fulfill Your Vows to the Lord?*

The Word of God teaches pledge offerings and vows to be made before the Lord. But notice what it says about these vows or pledges:

> **When thou vowest a vow unto God, defer not to pay it; for he hath no pleasure in fools: pay that which thou hast vowed.**
>
> **Better is it that thou shouldest not vow, than thou shouldest vow and not pay.**
>
> **Ecclesiastes 5:4,5**

There are other Scriptures which teach us concerning a vow, like Deuteronomy 23:21,22. It, too, says when you make a vow or pledge to God, you are to pay that vow.

When God moves upon your heart to pledge or to make a vow, you are to follow through and to fulfill that promise. If you don't, you are hindering the blessings of God that would be coming into your life.

4. *Are You Being a Good Manager of What You Already Have?*

Again, the question is not, "Lord, what do I need?" but, "Lord, what am I doing with what I have right now?"

In Matthew, chapter 25, Jesus teaches the parable of the wise managers, or faithful stewards. One individual received five talents, so he went and traded it, producing five more. (v. 16.)

There are people, especially in Full Gospel circles, who for some reason are afraid of business. They say, "I don't want to get involved with that. It may hinder some aspect of my life."

If you feel that way, you need to realize that God knows about business. When you seek Him about what to do with what you have right now, He can begin leading you into a process of trading, investing and multiplying what you have.

Now you have some valuable assets. Some people would immediately say, "Not me — my pockets are empty!" But money is not the only resource that you can convert into increase. What about your time? What about your talents?

I love to watch people fulfill the dream they have had to operate some particular business. Maybe their family or friends have tried to warn them against it. But they have stepped out by faith and have gone into business for themselves. They plan their work, then work their plan, converting their talents, their time, even their financial resources. By utilizing what God has given them, they bring increase in their lives as God prospers and financially blesses them.

If you are not seeing prosperity in your life, you need to ask yourself these questions: Am I utilizing all of the time and talents God has given me in such a way that they are being converted into extra income? Or am I always just sitting around, expecting God to channel blessings into my life?

Again, God teaches a strong work ethic. Are you always asking yourself this question: *Why isn't God blessing and prospering me?* If so, maybe it's because you are always sitting at home instead of involving yourself and converting what God has given you in the way of talents.

Some people have been given a tremendous amount of talent, but they don't ever use it. They just let it rust or collect dust. By doing so, they are limiting God and limiting themselves.

Start using what you have right now. Convert it over into a system of trading and management, and you will see God begin to bless you.

Many times Christians close the door on their blessings, because they are afraid to do something in the natural. They are afraid they will get things out of priority. They think they might miss something God wants them to do spiritually.

You need to realize that part of what God wants you to do spiritually is the converting of your own talents, abilities, time and resources. By doing this, you can be a greater blessing to God.

5. *Are You Neglecting God's Word in Your Life?*

The Bible teaches that as you plant God's Word in your life, it brings you prosperity as well. Psalm 1 says of this blessed person:

> **But his delight is in the law of the Lord; and in his law doth he meditate day and night.**
>
> **And he shall be like a tree planted by the rivers of water, that bringeth forth his fruit in his season; his leaf also shall not wither; and whatsoever he doeth shall prosper.**
>
> **Psalm 1:2,3**

We have read in Joshua 1:8 how, as the Word is in your mouth, it is meditated upon day and night and it is obeyed; then God will cause you to deal wisely in this life. It says: **...for then thou shalt make thy way prosperous, and then thou shalt have good success.**

So prosperity is also tied back to the Word of God and what you are doing with it in your life.

6. *Are You Pursuing the Dreams, Visions, Goals and Strategies God Has Given You in Life?*

Many people don't prosper because they fail to pursue the dream, the vision, the goal or the strategy that has been placed before them.

As Proverbs 29:18 says:

> **Where there is no vision, the people perish.**

This is true about people collectively, but it's also true of individuals personally.

I am constantly pursuing visions, dreaming dreams, setting goals and developing strategies.

Some people say, "But I'm afraid I will fail."

I would rather try and fail than just sit at home and never try. That's the biggest failure of all.

You need to pursue the dreams, visions, goals and strategies that God places within your heart.

7. Have You Been Negligent in Dealing With the Devil?

In Malachi 3:11 the devil, or Satan, is called **the devourer,** or the destroyer. Jesus described him in John 10:10 as always trying to steal, to kill and to destroy in our lives. James 4:7 says:

> **Submit yourselves therefore to God. Resist the devil, and he will flee from you.**

If you are not experiencing prosperity, or if you are having a hardship or a financial difficulty, you need to ask yourself these questions:

Am I submitted fully to God?

Am I really resisting the devil?

Am I using spiritual weapons — the shield of faith, the Sword of the Spirit and the name of Jesus — to stand against the devil?

Jesus said:

> **Whatsoever ye shall bind on earth shall be bound in heaven: and whatsoever ye shall loose on earth shall be loosed in heaven.**

> **Matthew 18:18**

You need to be taking authority over the enemy in your finances.

Someone once asked me, "It just seems like all hell is breaking loose in my life. What should I do?"

Stand up against that attack! And having done all to stand, stand therefore, using the whole armor of God. (See Eph. 6:13-18.) Take authority over it in the name of Jesus, and change your confession to what the Word of God says about your finances!

Conclusion

You have been brought into covenant with God through the blood of Jesus Christ. You have been made a citizen in His kingdom through the new birth.

I encourage you to work the principles that govern God's kingdom. This will bring supernatural increase into your life as you activate His covenant of prosperity.

Prayer

Father, in the name of Jesus, I thank You for Your Word. I just pray now that this reader will be, not just a hearer of Your Word, but a doer of Your Word.

I thank You that You desire to so bless Your people, that You take pleasure in the prosperity of Your servants, that You wish above all things that we would prosper and be in health, even as our souls prosper.

Lord, I pray that this reader will have a heart's desire to be a blessing to others, to have all sufficiency in all things in order to financially support every work of the Gospel.

I pray that You, Lord, would continue to encourage and stir within the heart of this reader to see Your prosperity come to pass in his or her life. In Jesus' name, I pray. Amen.

About the Author

Markus Bishop is the Senior Pastor of Faith Christian Family Church in Panama City Beach, Florida. Since 1993, Markus has taken the message of *Our Covenant of Prosperity* to the nation. Ministering on Kenneth Copeland's "Believer's Voice of Victory," as well as holding financial conferences across the country with Pastor Creflo Dollar, he has received hundreds of testimonies of how this message from God's Word has produced miracles in the finances of those who have put its principles to practice.

Markus' ministry focuses on the local church as he fulfills his call "to prepare God's people for works of service" (Eph. 4:12 NIV) and proclaims the message of deliverance and restoration to every area of life — spirit, soul, body, and financially. He encourages others to let the Bible be the final authority in their lives.

To contact Markus Bishop,
write:

Markus Bishop Ministries
P. O. Box 14121
Panama City Beach, Florida 32413

*Please include your prayer requests
and comments when you write.*

Additional copies of this book
are available from your local bookstore.

HARRISON HOUSE
Tulsa, Oklahoma 74153

The Harrison House Vision

Proclaiming the truth and the power
Of the Gospel of Jesus Christ
With excellence;

Challenging Christians to
Live victoriously,
Grow spiritually,
Know God intimately.